Copyright

Copyright © 2025 Anastasia Gargiulli
All rights reserved.
Cover photo by Chelsea Hindle

Born Blind. A Guide To Welcoming a Blind Dog Into Your Life

Born Blind. A Guide To Welcoming a Blind Dog Into Your Life

Anastasia Gargiulli

Contents

Copyright	i
Dedication	1
ACKNOWLEDGMENTS	2
1 About us	3
2 Introduction	12
3 The Preparations	15
4 The environment. Preparing your house	18
5 Basic cues	27
6 Coming home	42
7 Introducing your dogs	44
8 Equipment	49
9 Eye care	54
10 Settling in	58
11 Toilet training	60
12 Chewing	70
13 Resource guarding	76
14 Resting	79

15	Walking	82
16	Calming signals	87
17	Enrichment	94
18	Nutritional enrichment	97
19	Social enrichment	103
20	Physical enrichment	108
21	Sensory enrichment	111
22	Growing up	115
23	The end!	120
Resources and further reading		121
About the author		123

Dedication

To my family, who welcomed Jelly with open arms

ACKNOWLEDGMENTS

This book could not have been possible without the help of the wonderful people who so generously shared their experiences and advice with me.

Caitlin, Brian, Kat, and Vicki- I am incredibly grateful for trusting me with your words and thankful that we can share our beautiful dogs' stories to make a difference.

I also couldn't have done this without the support of my parents and my husband, who ensured I had time and space to write and supported me throughout the process.

1

About us

In this book, I have included the experiences of not just myself and my dog but also those of other wonderful people who have taken this journey. Their stories and advice are scattered throughout the book, so let's meet the incredible people with whom you will be sharing this journey.

Anastasia and Jellyfish

Anastasia is the author of this book, and she has never owned a blind dog before Jellyfish.

She saw his profile on Facebook, shared by a worried volunteer at a nearby rural pound, and adopted him a few days later. Jellyfish is a large mix-breed dog who absolutely loves life despite never having visually seen any of it. His joy for life inspires many around him, and his energy has brought Anastasia into the world of dog sports, where she competes with him in SprintDog and Scent work.

Anastasia wishes she knew that blind does not mean calm and quiet!

Jellyfish competing at SprintDog

Photo by Penny Parker

Hear No Evil – Australian Deaf Dog Rescue

Hear No Evil – Australian Deaf Dog Rescue (Hear No Evil) is a dedicated rescue group that specialises in raising awareness, rescuing, and rehoming special needs dogs, including those who are deaf, blind, or both.

Vicki has been a valued member of the HNE team for over six years and has played a vital role in helping rehome many incredible special needs dogs, including several blind dogs.

Huckleberry and Pocket. Vicki's deaf boys, who have been foster brothers to a couple of blind foster dogs

When blind dogs come into care, they often attract a lot of attention. They receive many wonderful adoption enquiries from people who are eager to give these dogs a loving home. But just as often, they also receive negative comments like "poor thing," or "they should be put down," and questions about how a blind dog could possibly live a good life.

The truth is, blind dogs are not broken or suffering. They are incredibly resilient, intelligent, and adaptable. With just a few simple accommodations, they can live happy, enriched lives just like any other dog.

At Hear No Evil, they don't see limitations—they see potential and stand firmly against the idea that a dog's life is worth less because they can't see.

Hear No Evil are also committed to supporting all dog guardians who share their lives with blind or special needs dogs. Whether you adopted through them or found your special friend elsewhere, they will provide support, guidance, and a community that celebrates the incredible value and capability of every dog.

Kat, Pepsi and Maisie

Pepsi was a black miniature poodle who came from a backyard breeder.

The breeders contacted Hear No Evil once they realised that Pepsi was blind.

Pepsi

He was 13 weeks old when Kat met him as a foster-to-adopt.

Pepsi was a crazy, excited little boy who loved to play with Kat and his adopted sister, Bella, the cavoodle.

He loved running, swimming, climbing, and was learning to jump through hoops!

Unfortunately, he suffered from epilepsy and passed at the age of one.

With the loss of Pepsi, Kat wasn't looking to adopt another blind dog. That was until her neighbours told her about a little dog who was in dire need of a safe home.

Maisie is a mini-Pomeranian who was used for breeding in a puppy mill for the first 3 years of her life, until she was dumped with an external hernia, and physical and mental scars that she still carries.

Maisie

Kat met her at a meet-and-greet at the shelter, where she was in an outside pen, looking scared and shut down. Maisie clicked with Bella, and they took her home that day.

Kat thought that raising blind dogs would be more difficult, that their blindness would be a challenge, and that they would struggle in the world. She was pleasantly surprised when she realised that both Pepsi and Maisie are normal dogs and can live their lives just as any other dog would. Kat wishes she knew that blind does not equal quiet.

Brian and Peter

Brian found out about Peter through a Facebook post, where he saw a video of him running in circles at his foster family's home.

Peter

Peter hadn't received a single application in two months, so despite Brian's lack of experience with blind dogs, he submitted one and was accepted!
He drove for nine hours to bring Peter home, where he now lives with his adopted brothers.
Brian wishes he knew that raising a blind dog isn't much more difficult than raising a dog who can see; it's so rewarding for you and your dog!

Caitlin and Freddy

Caitlin heard about Freddy from a colleague at Hear No Evil. Freddy was one of two blind toy moodles coming into care after being surrendered by their family due to health issues.

When he first came to Caitlin, Freddy was matted all over and needed a full body clip to remove the mats. He was born with microphthalmic eyes and needed to have one eye removed due to an injury that caused an infection.

Freddy

Her work in improving accessibility for people with disabilities had prepared her for raising Freddy to be similar. If he had typical canine cognition, she only needed to provide the necessary accommodation

2

Introduction

First of all, you are amazing. You are an incredible human being for even considering adopting a blind dog. I'm not sure what led you here, but I want you to know that I'm here for you and that you don't have to face this alone. Once you learn the ropes, raising a blind dog is a piece of cake. So, let's get on this ship and get all of our ropes in order (I've never been on a ship, I hope this metaphor works), because you're going to feel confident and resilient with the help of this book.

On the 8th day of 2024, my family and I went to a rural shelter to adopt a blind puppy. He was 18kg, 6 months old, and already had a failed adoption. I had no experience with blind dogs, having only had two dogs in my life who had a cocktail of other issues not relating to sight (severe reactivity, and health issues), I felt very out of my depth and remember thinking "What am I doing?" every day for the first 6 months that we spent together. I wouldn't say it was a disaster, but maybe it would have been easier if I had a guide I could rely on during this initial journey.

This is my aim with this book: to give you an easy-to-follow guide that covers all the essential aspects of raising a dog that is born blind. There are numerous free resources on the internet and in books about how to support a dog that has gone blind due to age, trauma, etc.

These resources are great if your dog was born with sight, but it's an entirely different situation if your dog was born blind.

Not all internet resources are reliable and trustworthy, and I had to comb through page after page to find helpful information. I hope that with this book, you won't have to do all that work, and you can spend that time enjoying your dog and getting to know each other.

Let's establish some ground rules before we proceed to the first chapter (the preparations).

I am not a dog trainer or behaviourist. Although I have worked with numerous professionals in the dog training field, the majority of the information in this book is either based on personal experiences of people who have raised blind dogs or on information from a rescue organisation.

Your dog may not be as hyper as mine, and she will have a different genetic makeup and life experiences. You will have to know your dog to be able to work with her. This book does contain aspects of basic training, but that's not the aim. The main goal is to set you up for success with your blind dog so that you can be confident in your abilities and go on and build a life that you and your dog deserve.

I will be using the words 'cues' and 'words' over 'commands' as I believe the words we use influence our perception of reality. Your dog may not understand or care for this difference, but it will affect how you ask or demand something of your dog and whether they have a choice to listen to it.

I will use "he" and "she" interchangeably throughout this book when talking about dogs. Boy and girl dogs exist, and it's not fair to stick to one pronoun and not include the other.

I don't know how old your dog is either, so I will use the words "blind dog" and "blind puppy" interchangeably.

The book's structure is mostly linear. We begin with the preparations needed before bringing your blind dog home, then move into settling your dog in, moving towards specific aspects of this, such as calming signals and enrichment, and finishing with what to expect of your dog as he becomes a teenager and an adult.

One aspect that I have not included in this book is socialisation. I do touch on this topic slightly in the social enrichment chapter; however, it is different to socialisation, as social enrichment is the continuation of a dog's already established socialisation level.

Your dog will already have some socialisation under his belt, depending on his age and life experiences, so it is my hope that the social enrichment section will help most dogs regardless of their socialisation skills.

I will include plenty of examples from my experience with my dog and personal stories of people and rescue organisations. My focus is to help you prepare and enjoy your life with your special dog.

3

The Preparations

Let's begin this chapter by focusing on what you can do *before* you bring your blind dog home.

Welcoming any pet into your home is exciting. Think of all the adventures that you will have together! There are many Christmases, birthdays, beach trips, and mountain hikes that I'm sure you're excited for. You are itching to meet your new best friend and make them fully a part of your family. Maybe you even ordered a custom collar with their name engraved on it and are already wondering if the colour will suit them.

All of this will come to be (within reason and depending on your dog), and you will have all the adventures with your new pup, but before doing so there is a bit of work to be done to ensure you are setting yourself and your new best friend for success from day one.

Let's start by going over the 3x3x rule. In case you haven't heard of the 3x3x3 rule, I have added an image that describes it below:

3-3-3 Rule, Humane Society of Ventura County, 2016

This rule applies to all dogs who are being rehomed, especially shelter dogs who are adopted and brought into a new home, perhaps even for the first time. It's important that we start here, by setting your expectations as low as possible. What I mean by this is that you can't expect your new dog to be cuddling up to you from the first day, know how to sit, wait for their food (if this is important to you), walk on lead, or even be toilet trained. This is especially true of special needs dogs.

When we adopted Jellyfish from the shelter, he was already 6 months old, and his background was unclear. All we know is that when he was approximately 4 months old, his family (presumably) drove onto one of the main highways in NSW and dropped him off on the side of the road. A car driving by saw what was happening and took Jelly in before anything could happen to him and brought him to the local shelter. He was then adopted and returned 2 weeks later, despite his new family doing everything they could to integrate him into their lives. Because of this, he was put on the euthanasia list and had 2 weeks left to find a home. Lucky for all of us, we spotted him online and made the decision to adopt him before we even saw him.

When we brought Jelly home, my expectations were at an all-time low for a few reasons, but mainly because I had just lost my dog after 11 years, and all I wanted was a companion. He wasn't toilet trained, the only cue he knew was 'sit', and he was a very over-aroused dog who I doubt knew how to settle (I'm sure it's quite hard in a shelter).

So, before we jump into how to live with your special puppy, I want to ensure that your house is prepared for what's about to come.

4

The environment. Preparing your house

The first step in preparing your house is to look at the layout of every room from the point of view of a blind dog. If you're really brave, I dare you to walk through your whole house and every room with your eyes closed. This will help you identify where the obstacles are for your pup and what needs to be moved for her to move freely.

If you are on the more sensible side, observe every room and try to remove unnecessary items, clutter, and even furniture. Move some of these to the edge of the room or even remove them entirely if they're not in use.

It is a complete myth that you won't be able to move your furniture with a blind dog. Why wouldn't you? Dogs that are born blind are not broken, and they don't need to be bubble-wrapped their whole lives. They may need a higher level of supervision and puppy-proofing in the initial stages, but there is no reason why you shouldn't be able to live your everyday life with your dog by your side.

However, I would not recommend moving the furniture in the first week, or even longer, if your pup needs more time to settle in. You want him to be comfortable in his new environment, to know it so well that he doesn't walk into the walls or the table.

Once he is walking around confidently, go ahead and move that couch! On this note, be prepared for him to walk into absolutely everything as he is settling in.

I can't give you a timeframe for this; it depends on your dog! All you need to do is be there for him and warn him before he walks into something.

Once you are happy with your layout, we'll cover up those corners and make sure any stairs you have are safe.

Corner covers are my favourite item for securing your house. They can be found in the baby section of most retail stores and online.

These are the surviving corner covers in our house, as some have been chewed off by Jelly when he reached adolescence. They are incredible things that come in a roll, so you can cut them to size and then stick them on any corner with the double-sided tape that is hopefully included in the box. You'll want to make them as tall as your dog is so that when they run into a corner with their nose, it won't hurt them.

They are not the most fashionable accessory in a house, but if you choose to include them, know that they are temporary and can be removed once your dog is older (or if they have developed a taste for ripping them off the walls).

The next thing we found to be even more helpful than the corner covers is mats!

I mean yoga mats, welcome door mats, bathmats, or any mats with different textures that you might even have lying around in your house already.

These are environmental cues, basically the house telling your dog, "Hey, there's a door here." This means you don't have to be following your dog 24/7 to tell them that there are stairs coming up or that he's about to walk into the kitchen.

Place these where you think your dog might get lost.

I would avoid putting them in front of bedrooms, bathrooms, and other rooms, as every room has a distinct smell that already tells your pup where they are.

A dog's nose is more powerful than ours. Now, imagine how powerful your blind dog's sense of smell is when they can't rely on their sight to gather information. When faced with your room, she will know where she is because of all the items in there. Your clothes, bedsheets, toys, personal items, and deodorant.

All of these will have a distinct smell that will tell her it's your room, the bathroom, or the guest room.

Having said this, if you believe that your new pup will benefit from having mats in front of the rooms, go ahead and put them down. You know your dog best, and it can't hurt to have them there. Just make sure that she won't slip on them. You can make them slip-proof by placing some yoga mats or grip mats that are used for cupboards underneath the mat.

On the topic of yoga mats, these can come in handy for your backyard as they are waterproof, have a great grip, and are generally long-lasting. The only issue with these is that they can be blown off from their designated area with high winds, and they're not very aesthetic (if you care about these things). I have mine on the top and bottom of the stairs, as well as in front of the doggy door and the sliding door, so that he knows which one he can open at any time. I choose to leave the mats in these spaces as Jelly often will run at full speed without any regard for his safety, and they are the only thing that will tell him where to stop. However, you can remove them after some time or remove some and leave a few, just like Caitlin and Kat chose to do. Once your dog has oriented himself comfortably around the house, you shouldn't need the mats unless you decide to leave them there.

It's entirely up to you and what your dog needs.

An alternative to these mats is Elastoplast. Caitlin used these with her dog Freddy to let him know which crate was his and which was his sister's. Elastoplast is absorbable and can stick to most surfaces long-term, so if you choose to put a few drops of essential oils on it, they will absorb the smell and can help your dog know where he is. This can be a temporary measure and should be faded off once your dog knows the layout of the house and where his specific areas are (if you choose to have any).

Your backyard (if you have one) is another area that will need to be inspected for safety. If you have any spiky plants such as cacti or rose bushes, you need to ensure your blind wonder pup won't be able to reach them. You can use chicken wire to surround the plants or move them to an area where only humans can reach them. Whatever you do, do *not* underestimate your dog!! I have found Jelly behind some very intricate and tough barriers in our garden, and once he even climbed the outdoor table. We still don't know how he did it!

If you compost, kudos to you, but you'll need to make sure your dog can't reach it. Compost has toxic elements that can cause serious illness if ingested by your pup. Remember that their sense of smell is incredible, and he *will* find that hole you dug for the compost.

Despite my best efforts, I have caught Jelly eating ibuprofen tablets, the compost, a spiky rose bush stem, raspberry bush leaves, a taste of my coffee, and many other items that he should not have in his system. This will most likely happen to you, too, despite your best efforts.

Please, please don't blame yourself. If anything happens, contact your local vet or an after-hours vet hospital for advice. Accidents happen, and raising a blind puppy does come with fun little adventures such as these.

I mentioned earlier how every room has its unique smell that tells your dog where he is. Well, here is one piece of advice that the internet loves to spread, which is simply not helpful. If you haven't heard of scent markers, they are items placed around the house that have a distinct smell and convey a specific message. For example, we got some toy stuffing and wrapped it in some fabric, which was tied close with a piece of string.

We then added some drops of lavender to the white ones and bergamot to the green ones. We hung the lavender ones on the top of the stairs, while the bergamot ones were for the bottom.

The theory is that the lavender smell will indicate that he's approaching a staircase that goes down. However, it can be placed in other parts of the house to indicate when they are about to reach a door, a room, etc. As explained earlier, these markers are unnecessary as your house is already full of these! We tried these out before bringing Jelly home and quickly realised they weren't helping him as he would rush past them and run up the stairs anyway.

When he could locate them, he'd take them for a play! If you do choose to try these out, remember not to overdo it on the essential oils, and make sure to do your research, as some oils can be toxic to your dogs if inhaled, and some if ingested.

They also need to be topped up every so often so that their smell doesn't evaporate, so keep a few bottles nearby and make sure your dog doesn't mistake them for toys.

Let's cover the stairs.

Stairs can be dangerous for your blind dog in the initial stages of getting to know his new environment.

To make this experience safer, invest in some adhesive carpet stair treads. The word is a bit of a mouthful, so simply put, they are just pieces of carpet with a sticky back that fit on your steps.

They give you and your pup grip, and the different textures available can be used to let your dog know when he's reached the top or bottom of the staircase.

We have some see-through treads on the top of every staircase, soft carpeted ones on the actual steps, and a large mat for the bottom. This variation in textures lets Jelly know precisely where he is on his stair journey.

If you want to avoid stairs altogether, there is no shame in blocking these off with a baby gate.

Lastly, let's discuss two more items that are often recommended for blind dogs: bells and crates.

Bells are recommended to be put on yourself (so that your dog knows where you are at all times), on the dog (so that you know where he is at all times), and on other family members, including any other pets. I have given this a go, and unfortunately, all the ringing from the bells drove us up the wall. Bells are as unnecessary as scent markers and don't provide any additional helpful information to your dog.

It might even make them feel overwhelmed and more confused because of all the extra stimuli.

Again, it's up to you if you want to try this method, so keep in mind the size of the bell, its location and how it's attached, so that your pup doesn't accidentally swallow it. Besides, one of the perks of having a blind dog is that you can (sometimes) sneak past them without waking them up!

Crates are a hot topic in the dog training world, so I won't spend much time on this. All I will say is that if you plan on using one, have it prepared and placed where you think your dog will find peaceful enough to sleep.

You might even want to cover it in a blanket to block out all light in case your pup has enough vision to distinguish day from night.

We originally had our setup include a crate where Jelly would occasionally sleep, but despite my best efforts, he never warmed up to it. We ended up working with him and removed the crate, choosing instead to proof the house to the max before leaving and making sure he had good house manners before letting him sleep free range at night.

5

Basic cues

With a blind dog, words are your friends. Words will replace hand gestures and body language, so you must be very careful with your tone and choice of words. You will want to set up a vocabulary before you bring your dog into your life. Trust me, we did it afterwards, and it was a mess trying to get everyone on the same page.

There are five people in our household, and for the first few weeks of having Jelly, we had accidentally been using the cues 'drop it' and 'leave it' to mean the exact same thing.

I can only imagine how confusing it must have been for Jelly!

If there are numerous people in your household too, make sure you are all on the same page and happy with the vocabulary you have chosen. Feel free even to print it out and put it on your fridge!

Having a blind dog with your sighted dogs can also be a blessing in disguise when it comes to communication. While dogs are quite visual, your blind dog will not know when you are giving visual cues to your other dogs, which can be beneficial if you are trying to ask different things of the dogs.

For example, Caitlin may use a visual cue to ask her sighted dogs to go to their beds so she can focus on Freddy, and he will not know that this has happened. She can also use touch cues with Freddy, and her sighted dogs will be none the wiser.

The way that you communicate with your pup will depend on whether your pup comes with a vocabulary already (both tactile and verbal), so it's very important that you enquire about this.

Marker word

Before we jump in and learn some helpful cues, it's important that you have an established marker word. A marker word is something that you say to let your dog know that they have done something good, and a reward is coming. For example, you see her going potty outside, so you say 'yes', ' good' or whatever your word is, and then follow it up with a game of fetch or a treat, whatever she enjoys.

Choose a marker word and stick to it. Make sure that everyone in your household uses the same word.

Before you do any formal training, it is often recommended to do something called marker loading. This is where you say your marker word and then follow it up with a reward.

They don't have to be doing anything; this exercise is to let your dog know what 'yes' means so that they know what to expect.

You won't have to reward your dog for every cue we will go through in this section (I will explain why very soon), but it's helpful to start thinking about and implementing to establish communication between you and your dog.

Careful

This word means that your dog is about to run into something. Say 'careful' if you see him heading for a wall or another stationary object. This training will most likely happen in a less formal way, for example, you won't be putting aside 5 minutes a day to formally go through this training, as it will happen more regularly than this!

Ideally, you will use this the first time you bring your dog inside your house. Let them explore on a lead, and when you see them about to walk into something, say 'careful' and hold the leash tighter to slow him down or stop him. Don't worry if you are too late with your cue, and he runs into that wall. Being born blind, they are more than used to running into stationary objects. They just shrug it off and move on! Having said this, please do exercise caution and common sense. Don't let them keep walking toward something dangerous and rely on your 'careful' to keep them safe. Teach this in a safe space, in a living room with couches and soft edges (thanks to the corner covers you already put out). The basic idea is that as soon as your pup hears the word, he will slow down and investigate what is in front of him with care.

You can take this further once they are proficient in this and include 'left' and 'right' to help them around an obstacle. To teach these, you can use treats to lure him left and right whilst saying the words. Then go outside on a walk and every time you turn left, say the word and then go slightly left, making sure there is some leash pressure so your dog can feel the leash tensing to the left. You don't have to do this right away. In fact, we didn't teach this to Jelly until he was at least 9 months old. It's not a crucial cue to learn like 'careful', so take things slow and add more cues when you and your pup are both happy with where you are.

If your house is a bit of a danger zone despite your best efforts, or you are very worried about the safety of your pup as she explores, you can use something called a halo.

A halo is a special type of vest made for blind and visually impaired dogs that has a round, plastic tube that is attached to the harness and comes up and sits around the dog's head.

It should sit just in front of the nose so that the plastic part of the halo touches the obstacle and not your dog's nose. This can be a great tool to build confidence in both you and your dog. However, it's not advisable to rely on it in the long term for several reasons.

The first one is safety. If you have brought home a blind puppy, leaving them with a halo can mean disaster for your house. Things can get caught and tangled in it, which can put your pup at more of a risk than if they were without a halo. They need to be constantly supervised if they have it on.

Secondly, your dog will learn to rely on the halo and will put in less effort to learn the layout of your house, as the halo is there to protect him. In the long run, this can mean that the dog will take longer to build up his confidence than if he wore his halo less, or not at all.

Hear No Evil doesn't advocate using halos for blind dogs as they can limit movement and make dogs less confident. Blind dogs navigate best by relying on their senses; a safe, consistent environment helps build their confidence without unnecessary restrictions.

Also, remember that this tool will restrict your dog's movements and allow them to have much less space than without one. It is also challenging to find the edge of a room or furniture with it on, and they may be unable to walk through doorways if you have a big dog with a big halo.

In general, they can be more stressful for your dog and even hinder their exceptional ability to orient themselves, making them less confident. Again, if you believe your dog would benefit from a halo, try it out; just keep an eye out for stress signals and any sign that your pup may be feeling less confident with it (we will go over these stress signals in Chapter 16, calming signals).

If you are interested in this, there are plenty of online tutorials on how to make a DIY one. Alternatively, they can be purchased online.

Jellyfish wearing his Halo, which is actually incorrectly fitted as it is too low!

Leave it

Depending on the age of your blind wonder, you will most likely come face to face with a land shark/vacuum cleaner that will chew on and swallow things he shouldn't. Most puppies and adolescents will go through a stage of tearing limbs off toys and eating them. Some breeds (I'm looking at you, Labradors) will always be at risk of this due to their genetics, so it's important to be vigilant and set your dog up for success.

The repercussions of not teaching them a solid 'leave it' can be dangerous for your pup, with the worst-case scenario being them needing a pricey surgery to remove the foreign object.

If the object is too big and can't be passed through their system, it can cause a blockage, which is painful and life-threatening to your pup. I don't want to scare you; this is the worst-case scenario, and often, small objects can pass through safely. Just stay vigilant and have your vet's contact details handy.

Jellyfish is my first blind dog, but not my first puppy, so I was surprised when I would watch him swallow his toy's limbs without a care in the world. He also swallowed a small rock once, thankfully, he was able to pass this too, but I am thankful every day that he is more mature now.

We chose the cue 'leave it' instead of 'drop it' as we use 'drop' to ask him to lie down, and as dogs don't focus on the whole word, and instead on the beginning, it would have been too confusing to use both.

To teach this cue, simply play with your pup using a toy. When you ask them to leave it, offer them a tasty treat so that they will let go of the toy. Keep practising this and swapping toys with other treats and items. Remember always to reward her when she leaves something with a treat or a game of tug, whatever she enjoys most!

A little bump that we faced when giving treats to Jelly was...how to give him treats. For a sighted dog, you offer them the treat and they can see you getting it out of your treat pouch, it being in your hand, and finally being close enough for them to take it. For a blind dog, they don't have this flow of information to let them know that a treat is coming, so it can be surprising for them when something yummy appears in front of their nose or is suddenly offered too quickly near their mouth. We overcame this by using a word and always giving him treats from under his mouth. He knows now that when we say, 'here you go,' he is expecting a touch on the chin and a treat in the hand.

Accidental cues and rewards

The cue 'here you go' was quite accidental, and I'm sure you will have a few of these cues too when teaching your blind dog. You don't have to put in any real effort to come up with a word and always repeat it with the correct action; I found that it happened so often that both Jelly and I were just used to it meaning a certain thing.

Another example of an accidental cue that we have is 'excuse me'. I started using this because I found it funny when he would stop right in front of me or block my path. He has since learned that 'excuse me' means he needs to move so people don't step over him or nudge him around to get past.

While the environment can be reinforcing and more useful when teaching some cues, such as 'careful', pairing a cue with treats or praise helps dogs learn more reliably, especially early in training.

Let me explain what I mean by this. When we say 'careful', Jelly slows down and investigates what's in front of him. His 'reward' is not walking into a wall. When I say, 'Excuse me,' he moves out of the way, and his reward is not being nudged around. With words like 'leave it', there is no environmental reward for leaving something your pup wants to chew on. The only reason he will leave this resource is for another even better one, hence offering him a treat or a game of tug.

Try to keep a few dry treats in your pockets to reward your pup when you see them performing a behaviour you like. For example, when they potty outside, lie down to rest, or leave an item they were chewing because you asked them to.

Up/Down

Some blind dogs fear using the stairs due to past experiences where they most likely fell down them. Make sure to keep the initial interaction positive and keep a leash on your dog when doing this for the first time.

If they won't use them, start at the bottom (if possible) and lure them up one step at a time using treats or a toy.

Reward them as soon as they show any interest in the step. If they sniff it, move closer to it, or even lift their paw: reward, reward, reward!

You want to build up his confidence and show him that he can do it all by himself, so go nice and slow and reward him like you're a Pez dispenser.

It's easier to start on the bottom of the stairs than from the top, but you can also do this exercise from the top, you'll just need to be very careful about it so they don't fall.

Use the words 'up' and 'down' when doing this exercise.

With sighted dogs, the advice is often to not give any cues when they are learning something new, for example, don't say sit until they know what you are asking them and introduce the word later. For blind dogs, you will need to use words while teaching the action so they don't get confused. So, say 'up' when your pup takes that first step up. You don't need to worry about this in the long run, but if she is worried about the stairs, then give her as many treats as she needs. Just remember to give her less dinner!

You can take this further when she has mastered the cues and moves on to unfamiliar stairs. Do this once she has completely settled down with you; otherwise, there is too much to learn at once.

When you are out for a walk, intentionally find some stairs or even use a curb to practice 'up' and 'down'. It helps to get their attention first by saying their name or a predictor word. You might have heard of a 'predictor word' before. All it means is that when you say this, your dog is expecting for something to happen.

For example, when we are walking, I will say 'ready...up'.

I do this because when I say Jelly's name, I want him to come to me and pay attention to me. When I say 'ready', I want him to expect another cue to follow, so he needs to concentrate and listen for that cue and not be lost in the wonderful world of smells and sounds. So in this case, 'ready...' is my predictor word.

This is a helpful exercise as you never know when you and your pup will need to face unfamiliar stairs in the world. When you start looking for them, stairs are everywhere!

At the vet's office, the groomer, puppy training classes....

Of course, if your blind pup happens to be small enough to be able to pick up, you can avoid doing this training (although I would still recommend doing it). You will have to come up with a word before you pick them up too so that they know to expect it.

Recall

Recall training is the same with a blind or sighted dog; the only difference is that you need to be vigilant about your surroundings and not stand behind a bush when you call your pup. Additionally, unlike sighted dogs, where the standard recommendation is to cue the dog once and not repeat it again, it is necessary to repeat yourself with a blind dog so that they can locate you, especially with a recall cue. You can also use finger clicking to have your dog locate you, just as Caitlin does to indicate where she wants Freddy to go so he can follow the sound to find her.

Start by holding something that your dog enjoys, a squeaky toy, a tug toy, or a yummy snack. Watch your dog; when they are not busy sniffing or playing with something, call their name and squeak that toy! If they don't come straight away, you can repeat their name gently to help them localise you – just avoid turning it into a nagging call.

When you have both mastered this at home, take it outside and practice this on a leash on your walks, or in a safe off-leash park. You don't have to limit yourself to only saying his name once, as commonly recommended for sighted dogs. Your blind dog will hear you once, but to help him locate you, keep saying his name until he finds you, especially if you are in an unfamiliar environment that he finds distracting.

A tip on food rewards

Food rewards are the easiest and most efficient rewards you can use when training your pup. They don't have to be expensive gourmet treats; they can be some of her kibble or dehydrated chicken you made at home.

Other high-value treats can be: cooked chicken breast, beef, tuna, peanut butter, pizza crust, whipped cream, pieces of apple/banana/pear, etc. You can get really creative with what rewards you use!

A fun game to play with your dog to find out what treat they prefer is to offer them two or more different treats and see which one they go for first. Whatever they choose first will be of higher value to them than the other treats.

For example, Jelly loves cooked chicken breast but always chooses pizza crust over it. This means I can give him the higher value treat (pizza crust) during more stressful events, such as a vet visit or an ear clean.

Examples of more cues

I don't want to overwhelm you with this section of cues, so if you are feeling a little confused or overwhelmed, please feel free to skip the rest of this section and move on with the rest of the book. You can always come back to this!

I decided to add a few more cues that we use in our everyday lives with Jelly, which I hope can help you.

Of course, you don't have to use any of these, and you can always change the words and add your own cues that fit your lifestyle.

Go find
We use this to tell Jelly that there are treats scattered on the ground and that he needs to put his nose to the ground and concentrate on the smells. This can come in handy if you want to get into scent work someday or if your pup needs a distraction from a trigger.

Search
Search refers to finding a specific object, such as a toy or clothing, hidden nearby. It does not refer to food, as that would be too confusing with the cue 'find it'. This can be useful if you ever want to do tracking work with your dog or have him find your lost objects.

Wait/Stay
Both words mean the same thing, so choose one and stick to just that one. We use 'wait' to ask Jelly not to move while we open a door, pick up his poop on a walk etc. You can also use this to mean stop or have 'stop' as your cue. This has to mean something different from 'careful', so make sure you teach him the difference.

Who's there?
This means that someone from our household is about to walk in, and Jelly doesn't have to alert bark. I appreciate his barking when he

hears someone trying to enter our house, but it must also be annoying being so worried every time this happens. We've come up with 'who's there' so that Jelly doesn't have to worry about letting us know of a potential burglar. Instead, we let *him* know that it's okay and it's someone we know. We often follow it up by "it's___ (person's name)" to let him know exactly who is coming in.

Naming body parts

This comes in handy when we have to do treatments on him, such as an ear clean or a nail trim. Start by saying the body part that you are about to touch, for example, "ear" and then touch one of his ears. I decided not to differentiate between left and right ear and found that Jelly does well with this, but you are welcome to change it up and see what works for your pup.

Jelly is quite touch-sensitive, most likely due to his blindness. It must be scary not knowing when someone is about to touch you, and you don't even know where!

To counter this, try saying the body part you are about to touch before patting him, or even say 'pat' to warn him.

If he finds any interaction uncomfortable, stop and reassess the situation. Make sure he feels uncomfortable because of the touching and not because of something else, so that you don't try to change something that doesn't need to be changed. Feel free to reward your pup after you touch a sensitive area. For example, Jelly has sensitive ears, so we use plenty of food rewards during an ear clean. Remember that your dog doesn't have to love having treatments done on him; it's okay if he can just tolerate it.

Naming toys

Similarly to naming body parts, you can name his favourite toys and see which one he prefers playing with at that moment. Our favourites are tug and ball, and I will say 'more?' if he is running around with the ball in his mouth to ask if he wants me to throw it. If he does, he will come back and give it to me. If he doesn't, then he wants to be chased and play tug with the ball. For context, his favourite ball is the Kong Jumbler, which has handles on either side of the ball for tug play, and a ball on the inside which makes a noise so it's easy for Jelly to locate it.

Watch out!

I use this when my other dog, Clyde, indicates he wants to play with Jelly. Clyde does this by crouching or by staring intently at him, which, of course, doesn't help my blind dog understand what's happening.

To help Jelly with this, I will whisper, "Where's Clyde?" which is his cue to look for Clyde, who most definitely wants to play right now. When he's close, or when I see Clyde getting ready to tackle him, I will say "Watch out!", so Jelly has time to brace and hopefully figure out where he will be tackled from. They will then happily wrestle and chase together.

There are no limits to what your blind dog can learn and what you can do with this knowledge. For example, you can teach your dog the 'touch' cue, where they touch their nose to your hand, and then extend it to objects like a bell.

This is precisely what Caitlin did with Freddy. She built on his understanding of 'touch' by introducing a rose scent to the ball at the end of her click stick. Once he learned to associate the smell with the cue, she transferred the scent to a bell, which he now touches when he needs to go outside.

Day/night confusion

Another little thing that might need to change in your household is the day and night routine. For a completely blind dog, it can be challenging to know when it's daytime, and as such, when it's acceptable to play and engage with the rest of the family, and when it's nighttime, which is not the time to make a bit of a ruckus.

Kat's dog, Maisie, faces this challenge daily and chooses to play with her toys in the early morning when everybody is asleep. Maisie tries to wake Kat up to play with her, but as not many are willing to play at 1 a.m., Kat tells her that it's sleep time, and Maisie plays on her own.

Jellyfish used to wake up at 6 am and start going through his energy supply by chewing the couch, walls, and his toys (and sometimes trying to swallow them). Until he learned to sleep for more extended periods of time and what his appropriate chews were, we had to wake up with him and supervise him. This may be a more straightforward process if your pup is crated during the night, but it doesn't guarantee that she won't wake up at 6 am needing the toilet or an outlet for her energy.

We started an evening enrichment routine to help Jelly understand when it was time to wind down. At around 6-7 p.m., we would get some puzzles, toilet paper rolls, snuffle mats, and boxes and hide treats in them. They weren't too hard to solve, but it would take him approximately 20 minutes to find them all, by which time he was relaxed and mentally tired—and ready for bed!

After a few months of this, we stopped doing it so regularly as his body clock had adjusted enough to fit in with our routine.

Your routine could look entirely different for this; there are many things you could do to indicate that it's time to settle. You could use a settle cue, give him something to chew on that he only has before bed, bring out his night-time bed or crate, put on specific pre-bed relaxing music, etc. I'm sure you could even turn the TV on when you're relaxing in the afternoons, and that could be enough of a signal.

Whatever you choose, make sure that you stick with it. If you choose your cue to be relaxing music, you can't then change it to heavy metal music after a few weeks and expect your pup to understand this. Create a routine that is easy for you to implement long-term, or indefinitely if needed.

6

Coming home

When your pup comes home for the first time, please keep your hands off them as much as possible. I mean this in both a physical and abstract sense.

Imagine being blind, brought into a new place with strange people, and suddenly, hands are touching you all over. You don't know where they are coming from or where to expect them next. Some hands might even be hurting you due to your sensitive skin.

You don't know where you are and are trying hard to make sense of your new environment, but the touching and chatter of new people distracts you. How frustrating does that sound? Even extremely social dogs who love people will need a hands-off approach while settling in.

Try to minimise patting, just let them know when you are about to touch them and soon, they will learn what that word means.

Also, try to minimise loud noises, which can be tricky if you have a large family and young children. High-pitched noises can be extremely stimulating, and your blind dog will not benefit from them in these early stages.

This is why Hear No Evil advocates for keeping your dog's world small initially. There will be plenty of time to let them roam around the house and play with your family. Your dog just needs time.

You can implement this by using some of the tools outlined earlier (gates, barriers) or by placing them in one room of the house and keeping them there for an initial two weeks. When your dog is more comfortable navigating his surroundings, you can expand the space by placing a pen around the front of the room, so they have more access.

Do this once a week, expand their knowledge and comfort of the house by making their space bigger, but remember that all dogs are different, and some may need more time in their initial space, and some might not tolerate it at all.

Try to give your dog time to rest and decompress but also go in and spend some time together playing or just sitting in the same space. It will be beneficial to only let a select number of people do this with your new dog to create a sense of security. This way, they will have someone to trust while they navigate the rest of your house and family.

The layout of your house will also impact how you can achieve this. You have to remember that the area your dog is confined to needs to be big enough for them to be able to sleep on one side, eat, and toilet away from each area.

Kat set Maisie up in her laundry when she first brought her home. The initial two weeks were spent decompressing in the room and getting used to the sounds and smells around her. With her other dog, Pepsi, Kat used a soft playpen, which allowed her sighted dog Bella to interact with him at a distance.

7

Introducing your dogs

I have no doubt that somewhere in your research, you have accessed social media accounts that have shared heartwarming videos of a sighted dog leading a blind dog by his leash. Stories like these are numerous and quite beautiful, but they don't always portray the reality of the situation. For the most part, the blind dogs in these videos were sighted once, and it is a much scarier world to live in if you were able to see and then lost this ability. This is why much of the information that is commonly accessible will have this kind of dog in mind, the one that lost his sight, not the one that never had any.

Your blind dog (depending on his history and eye issues) has never seen daylight or what the moon looks like, or if you prefer not to shave your leg hair. Since they were born, they had to learn how to move around in the world with only their other senses, so they will most likely be incredibly confident, if not a little wary in the beginning (hopefully!). Depending on their background and early life experiences, they were probably alone and didn't have another dog to 'guide' them through the various life experiences. Sometimes, even humans miss that one of the puppies is blind, especially if they were born with seemingly healthy and normal eyes. It's incredible how many people miss the fact that Jelly is blind despite having no eyes!

I often have to point this out to them when asked if he is vision impaired.

In my personal experience, you will not need to adopt a seeing-eye dog for your blind dog. If you are worried about him walking into things or not knowing that there are obstacles in his way, that's where you and your preparation skills come in. If your house is set up safely for a blind dog, and you are around in the beginning stages and on every walk with him to guide him, he'll be just fine!

However, if you already have another dog at home, there are some things that you can do to introduce them safely.

It can be hard for sighted dogs to make sense of the behaviour of blind dogs, their strange gait, constant bumping into things, and play can be confusing. Be prepared for your sighted dog to feel this confusion and allow them plenty of space and opportunity to move away from your blind dog.

There is an incredible variety of barriers, pens and gates that can be used when introducing a new dog to the household.

Hear No Evil advises to keep the world small initially for your blind dog as it can be overwhelming for a new dog to suddenly find themselves in a new house, with new people, and even new dogs. This is even more overwhelming for a blind dog, as they have to make sense of their new world with their other senses and by trusting you to keep them safe.

Although this method is effective and safe, there are times when it may be challenging to apply.

Our house's layout meant that we could not confine Jellyfish to just one area. His incredible energy and history of abandonment twice in his young life meant that he couldn't be left alone. We couldn't close any doors (bathroom, bedroom, etc.) without him becoming distressed, causing him to whine and jump on the door.

In his early life, Jelly was adopted by a well-meaning couple who, unfortunately, were only able to keep him in a designated area on their deck. Despite the safety that it provided, Jelly was distressed by this isolation, especially as he values human interaction highly and finds it comforting.

I can only imagine his fear of being abandoned a third time, which is why we opted to have him free-range in the house from day one. At this stage, he was the only dog in the house, with only five adults living in it. He was and still is everybody's shadow.

He is the one who will wait outside the bathroom door for you, who will lie by the bed until you wake up, and who will wake up from his nap if you decide to go to the kitchen for a snack. To him, confinement of any type is aversive due to his trauma. Because of our house's layout and adult family members, it was safer to let him explore the environment without any restrictions. I can imagine it would have been overwhelming to him, but also much less aversive than keeping him confined.

It is entirely up to you how you choose to introduce your blind dog to your home and family members. You can begin by keeping them in a room or a soft pen and see if they are happy in it. You can let them explore the house free range but always monitor them for signs of stress and have a plan for how you might help them feel more comfortable. If your lifestyle allows you, you can choose an in-between method and keep him on a leash for the first few weeks. He can come with you around the house and is always supervised. There are some things to consider with this method, specifically the lack of autonomy your pup will experience. You should only use this method in the early stages of acclimating your dog to your house.

With Jellyfish, we accidentally adopted a second dog only 2 weeks after adopting Jelly. This was not planned at all, and it was an incredibly stressful time for everyone involved.

Our second dog, Clyde, needed to be urgently moved on from his foster home. And as we were originally looking at adopting him before we came across Jelly, we decided to foster him for a short time until a long-term foster home presented itself. Fortunately for all of us, Clyde was the perfect piece in our family puzzle, and we officially adopted him after fostering him for five days!

Clyde

I would not recommend doing this; it was absolute chaos for about 6 months. If we didn't have the experience that we did with tricky dogs, we would have been faced with some tough decisions and possibly even considered rehoming.

Jelly wasn't toilet trained yet, we were just getting to know each other, he didn't know how to rest and was learning the day/night routine. Clyde came to us mostly toilet-trained, having had only one accident in the house. Still, he was fearful of loud noises and the men in the household, which often led to him running into the backyard and sitting under a tree for hours before being comfortable enough to come back inside.

Both boys had so much to learn, and everyone in the household also needed to be on the same page with their training, which was perhaps the most challenging part.

In the end, Jelly took Clyde under his wing and gave him the confidence he needed to learn to trust us.

Personality played a big part in our success story, and we are so lucky that Clyde is so patient and calm with Jelly.

Kat's sighted dog, Bella, was only 2 years old when Pepsi came into the picture. She was already a calm dog who helped test the personalities and behaviours of foster dogs in the rescue she volunteers with.

When Brian introduced Peter to his sighted brothers, he opted not to use any tools or barriers due to his dogs' calm personalities. Peter was able to map the house by brushing against things or running into them.

Whatever your circumstances, matching your dogs' personalities is one of the most important things you can do to prevent your household from becoming chaotic.

Disclaimer note: While calm introductions can work well, always supervise early dog interactions and consider using gates or crates if needed to ensure everyone feels safe.

8

Equipment

There are some talented people who are making incredible equipment for blind dogs, which can help raise awareness of your special needs pup.

These include leash sleeves, bandanas, harnesses, collars, and vests. It is up to you if you want to display your dog's blindness or if you prefer that people don't know about it.

For safety reasons, some people choose not to disclose their dog's blindness when they are walking due to the unsafe area they live in.

Jellyfish with his leash sleeve

If you are in a relatively safe area and wish to have these warnings on your dog, they can help deter people from approaching him and startling him with interactions such as patting. They can also help if your pup is an escape artist, so the finders don't have to struggle too much to determine if your dog has been hurt in his escape.

Freddy wearing his 'blind dog' harness

In my personal experience, I use leash sleeves on my everyday walks and bandanas on some occasions where I expect there to be a bit more of a crowd. I have found that people will be more careful and try to read what the leash sleeve says, during which time you can decide if you want your pup to say hello to them or just move on. I prefer to have these labels exactly for that, just to buy me some time to judge the situation.

Kat advocates for Maisie by using custom wording on her pram. She was frequently judged and criticised for not having her dog walk on a leash, and people assumed that she was old and unable to walk.

Maisie in her pram

With the sign, she has found people to be less judgmental and more able to start conversations about blind dogs and their differing needs in life.

There are plenty of local and online shops that sell this equipment, as well as custom-made ones, so you can edit the wording to suit your needs.

One piece of equipment that is not recommended for any special needs dog, especially a blind dog, is an electric collar. Hear No Evil also advocates against the use of them, as a blind dog's sense of touch is heightened and even on the lowest of settings, can be aversive to their well-being.

It can cause anxiety, as the dog won't know what the vibration is in relation to and how he can stop it.

Generally, people choose to use electric collars for deaf and blind dogs to 'keep them safe' while they are off lead.

This is not only unnecessary but also detrimental to the dog's well-being and sense of security.

As not all dogs can be trusted to be off-leash, long lines are a much safer option to use to give your dog more freedom while also keeping them safe.

Alternatively, visiting an enclosed area where your dog can run off-lead can also give your dog freedom of movement without using any tools.

9

Eye care

You have made it to Chapter 9, congratulations! I hope you have picked up a few helpful tips throughout the book so far and feel more prepared to welcome your blind dog home.

In the next chapter, we will review some helpful things you can do when you bring your dog into your life. Before we move on, I would like to give you one more piece of advice.

If your blind dog has eyes, you will need to be very careful with them to keep them trauma-free. Because she can't see, she will most likely run into things that can be sharp and potentially cause damage to her eye. You can't bubble wrap the entire house and garden, but when you think you're completely ready, have another walk through all areas of your home and look for anything that might damage an eye. Sticks in the bushes, sharp bench/chair corners, even the Christmas tree can be dangerous!

When Jelly was 7 months old (1 month after we adopted him), his left eye turned blue. We rushed him to the vet, where they measured his eye pressure and looked for any ulcers or cuts in the cornea. His eye pressure was at 50, nearly triple what it should be. At 9 months old, the same thing happened to his right eye and his pressure that time hit the 60s! Jelly had developed glaucoma. All of this means that the fluid pressure in the eyes had built up and was causing him pain. If he had any vision, it would have been severely compromised by this point, and he would have become blind. We treated his left eye with eye drops to reduce the pressure, as well as pain killers for the pain that he was experiencing, until he had his surgery to remove the eyes.

Dogs don't tell us where and when they are experiencing pain, and with Jelly, it was even harder, as we had only known him for a month before this happened. We noticed he was more over-aroused than usual and had more trouble settling down during the day. He would paw at his eye sometimes, and most importantly, he became head shy.

This is where the dog shows clear dislike for being patted on the head, which was unusual for Jelly at that point. If your dog has *any* changes in his personality or habits (eating, drinking, sleeping, toileting, playing), assume that he is at the very least feeling uncomfortable, if not experiencing some pain.

Unfortunately, blind dogs are even more predisposed to eye issues, especially if they were born blind. Genetic, hereditary, and developed issues can affect the eyes, so it's important to keep them safe.

Some people will train their blind dogs to wear goggles when they go for a walk to prevent anything from hurting their eyes. If you let him off lead one day, the goggles will provide more safety for his eyes, even when he is far from you. The main thing to remember with this equipment is that not all dogs will like it! Like a muzzle, you will need to train him to tolerate it and not take it off. Start slow, reward often; before you know it, he will keep his eyes safe all on his own.

Freddy wearing his eye protection

If you are wondering what we did to treat Jelly's glaucoma, the answer is that there is no treatment, and we had the eyes removed. This is because glaucoma treatment in animals (and people) focuses on retaining sight. Since Jelly already had none, there was no point in keeping the eyes and putting everyone through four rounds of eye drops, twice a day. The enucleation (eye removal) surgery is very straightforward; I recommend chatting to your vet if you think your dog might need it.

Not all blind dogs with eyes will face problems. Maisie, for example, has one microphthalmic eye (abnormally small) and one that bulges out of her eye socket. She has no pupils, and so far, has had no issues with her eyes. If your new pup has eyes, keep a close eye on them (yes, the joke was intentional) and help them stay out of trouble.

And with that, you are ready to jump into Chapter 10!

Let's learn how to toilet train, prevent your couch from getting chewed apart, teach your pup how to rest, and have a solid foundation for acceptable social skills (greeting others, walking on leash).

10

Settling in

This chapter is about how you can make life easier for yourself and your new pup.

You must be over the moon to have finally brought home your special new best friend!

Now that your new friend has come home, I can imagine that he will do quite a few things that are not socially acceptable behaviours for dogs in our society. Let's remember that dogs have needs that often vastly differ from ours, and they will try to meet those needs in whatever ways they can, so it's essential to teach them how to meet those needs safely.

If you have a confident blind puppy who is not afraid to explore the world and run full speed around a new place without *any* regard for consequences, I can relate.

Let's take a big breath together. It will be okay.

The timeframe for learning anything new will depend on several factors, including how consistent you are with your teaching, how often he is able to rehearse wanted and unwanted behaviours, and how you teach it.

Studies continuously find that children learn much faster if it is done through play (Skene et al., 2022, Weisberg et al., 2016). Now, I don't know of any similar studies relating to dogs, but we do know that full-grown dogs have the mental capacity of a 2-year-old (breed dependent), so it's fair to assume that they, too, will learn faster if it's done through play.

It will be an incredible journey, but before we begin, let's keep in mind that your puppy is in this world for the first time, so if he's doing something that you don't like, please don't punish him—he just doesn't know what else to do! You'll be doing a lot of teaching, so don't forget to take time for yourself and ask for help when you need it.

11

Toilet training

Puppies are hard work; perhaps the most challenging part of raising one is toilet training. You will have accidents in the house, maybe even on the furniture. However, with time, patience and consistency, this period won't last long.

Jelly came to us from a rural shelter, and the one time he was adopted, he was kept in an enclosure outside. Both times, there was no possibility to start toilet training, so when he came to us, this concept was quite foreign to him.

It can be more difficult for shelter dogs to be toilet-trained because they don't often get the chance to practice this in the kennels.

This can be considered a self-rewarding behaviour, as the act of toileting would feel good to a dog, so it didn't matter if they had to do it in their kennel. In short, they reinforced the behaviour themselves because they had no alternative, and because peeing feels good. It's helpful to remember this when teaching them where to go to the toilet.

Adding to this, we didn't know what kind of food he was given at the shelter, so we had to feed him our choice of food without any transitioning. The transitioning process from one type of food to another is incredibly important for a puppy.

Their digestive system needs time to process the new food, and if they don't have this time...let's just say it can get quite explosive. So, we had a blind puppy in a new home who wasn't toilet trained and had runny poos.

I did some research before getting Jelly on how others have toilet trained their blind dogs, and there are quite a variety of ways you can do this. You can use leads, crates, barriers, special words, and a strict schedule. You do not need anything special, such as flowers, scents, wind chimes or candles to let them know where the outside is and where they need to go to the toilet. Your pup's sense of smell is exceptional; they can pick up the scent of where they (or another dog) have toileted and assume that it's acceptable to go. If you have another dog in the house who isn't 100% toilet trained, you can do more training with them to help them, but make sure to use an enzyme cleaner in the meantime. These are usually named 'urine remover' and can be found in pet shops and online. They remove the enzyme smell which dogs can pick up but is odourless to our noses. If the indoors don't smell like urine, but your backyard does, they will prefer to go outside. Unfortunately, it's not always that simple. The above is just one piece of the puzzle in the toilet training game.

Human babies and toddlers are not born toilet trained, and the research tells us that they need to learn to make the connection between their bodies telling them they need to go to the bathroom and them consciously choosing to walk over to it instead of just toileting wherever they are. (Mahler, 2017). This connection is called interoception, and is also something that puppies and young dogs need to make, and we can help them with this.

Generally, when dogs put their noses to the ground and start to smell around them, that's your cue to take them outside. With a blind dog, it gets a little bit trickier, as their noses are always working!

You will need to be extra vigilant with your supervision so that you can succeed. So, start here. Observe your new puppy and watch for any different behaviour that they display when they are about to go to the toilet.

Does she spin in a circle, sniff very intensely despite having her toy nearby, or walk around seemingly aimlessly? These are just some of the behaviours we observed in Jelly, which helped us know when he needed to go.

Another helpful thing you can do is take your pup out regularly to the toilet. This can be as often as every 1-2 hours if they're very young. However, make sure you are not disturbing their sleep, as puppies need a lot of sleep to grow! A good rule of thumb is to take her out as soon as she wakes up, before bed, after a meal, and regularly throughout the day.

You can do the above and go a whole day without any accidents indoors; however, for this to succeed, you need to be watching your dog all day. You can share this load with other household members if they agree, just make sure they are all doing the same thing, or your pup might get confused and not understand what is expected of him.

A secured area can be helpful if you can't watch your dog all day, and crates are not the only option for keeping dogs in a safe area. You can create a safe area for your dog to be when they can't be supervised in an X-pen; the only difference is that it's less constricting and not completely escape-proof.

Example of an x-pen

Shutterstock

Crate training is a useful skill for emergencies; however, if it's not vital to your everyday life, you can focus on it later in your journey. Consider using x-pens or baby gates if you need to restrict your dog's movements.

This area should feel safe to your dog, so make it cozy and fill it with things that won't harm them, such as a dog bed, some safe chews, and toys if you believe they can be left with them and not eat them. It's generally easier to train your dog to be happy in an x pen rather than a crate, but do take the training slowly and consistently, and never leave your dog in a confining area if they are distressed.

Crates and x-pens can be used in the toilet training journey as they can spend time there to rest (while you're at work, for example) and then be free range with you once you can supervise them again and continue the toilet training.

They may have accidents there too, but generally dogs won't toilet where they sleep (although shelter dogs often have no choice, so they may continue doing this at home).

Crates are not necessary if you choose not to use them; in fact, several countries have banned or restricted their use (Finland and Sweden), so we can safely assume that they have found other ways to train their dogs (DogZone, 2022).

If you struggle to supervise your puppy but don't want to use the crate, you can follow Dr Sophia Yin's method in her book, "Perfect Puppy in 7 days: How to start your puppy off right". In this book, Dr Yin suggests putting your new puppy on a leash and have them with you at all times during the day. This way, there is less of a chance for them to have accidents because they are right next to you, so you can spot the signs right away. This doesn't have to be something permanent; it's designed to quickly teach your dog where to toilet so they can then have freedom around the house.

Both of the above options work by having physical control over your dog, which is something that may or may not work in your situation.

I felt uncomfortable using either of these options with Jelly as I wanted him to remain his confident and happy self, but also make good choices. With another puppy, I might have given these a chance, but I knew it would do more harm than good with Jelly.

I believed that if I were to restrict his movement too much, he would become frustrated and lose his independence and confidence. If any advice ever feels wrong to you, you don't have to do it.

You don't have to please your best friend's sister's husband because he had a dog once, and this is how she toilet-trained him. Likewise, if any advice you read in this book doesn't sound like a good fit for you, don't do it!

You will find your own way, which might be one that isn't common or entirely unique for you and your dog. I believe in you, and I have complete confidence that you can do this.

We were given quite a bit of advice by people with experience with visual impairment and blindness.

However, we did it our way, and we had Jelly toilet-trained in under 2 months. The general rule is that a dog can be considered completely toilet trained if they don't have accidents indoors for at least two months straight, so don't be discouraged if this process takes this long or even longer. It will be worth it, and I hope that you can enjoy the journey.

How we trained Jelly isn't unique, but it was incredibly effective. We used supervision and rewards in the form of treats or play. We also included special words such as 'go outside' and 'go pee pee'. I will go over these in more depth very soon.

We supervised Jelly all day, every day. At night, he would sleep with us on the bed, and we would close the door. If he needed the toilet, he would whine or jump on the door, so one of us had to get up and take him outside.

This worked well for the nights as he never toileted in our bedroom, but the days would be trickier. I had to pause my hobbies and studies because Jelly didn't know how to rest. Having come from a shelter where dogs would bark all day and people would come and go, I can imagine how difficult it must have been for him to find some peace and quiet during the day.

His inability to rest meant that he was always doing something.

Whether it was walking around and exploring the house, chewing on something or playing with a toy, someone was always supervising him. This was also helpful as we could teach him other useful cues, such as 'leave it' (he explored everything with his mouth!) and recall.

When we noticed the subtle changes in body language before he toileted, we would say 'go outside' in an excited (but not too high-pitched) tone and quickly lead him out. We kept the experience positive and made it into a game.

His reward for going to the toilet outside was always something he loved—either a tasty treat or a quick game. Sometimes we had to be patient once we got outside, as he'd often get caught up in all the exciting smells or dive straight into playtime instead.

But when he eventually did go, we'd gently say "go pee pee" while he was peeing so he could start associating the cue with the action.

That cue really came in handy later on, especially in new places like a friend's house or at the vet, when I needed him to go on cue.

Of course, we weren't perfect and occasionally missed his "I need to go" signals. If we caught him mid-pee indoors, we'd calmly interrupt and guide him outside to finish. I'm sure that must've been a bit frustrating for him, but I think even that helped reinforce the idea that toileting happens outside, not inside.

Damage control

Let's look at some common issues that arise when toilet training a new puppy and how we can work through them.

When I was a young adult raising my first dogs, I relied on family, friends, and other adults in my life to help me with basic training. Looking back, I realised how harsh and damaging some of that advice was, and unfortunately, some of it is still very much in circulation around the world. Some of this advice would be so detrimental to the dogs' trust in their humans that they would regress in their toilet training education because of it.

Let's imagine for a minute that you are a young child, maybe around the age of 2, who has been adopted by a family who don't speak your language and look very strange. You quickly observe that they have structures, routines, and acceptable behaviours that are tolerated and encouraged, but you don't understand it all. Where you come from, you had different rules and are not used to eating at a set time every day, eating a different kind of food, and toileting wherever smelled good! This is unacceptable in your new family, and they get so mad when you wee on the carpet that their behaviour scares you. This behaviour is scary and confusing. You think they don't like it when you do it in front of them, so you try to hide when you go to the toilet, so they don't get mad at you. This doesn't work, and now you're even more scared and confused! They put you outside, but you don't know why. You keep toileting inside because you don't understand what is expected of you, and you now don't trust your new family that much.

This is a very common situation that occurs in some households. Punishment and fear should never be a part of a dog's training plan, including when they are learning to become toilet-trained. These aversive techniques will result in your dog hiding from you, leaving wee puddles behind the couch, and not trusting you. They are not doing this out of spite (an emotion they cannot feel); they're confused. This is even scarier for your blind dog, and trust is even more important with them.

If you are already in this situation, it's not too late! It may take a little time for your dog to trust you again. This is all just a case of miscommunication, so all you need to do is communicate your expectations clearly and show him how to achieve them. Use rewards, be consistent, and take a deep breath when it goes wrong.

This is a long process, and you are bound to get stressed and lose your cool sometimes (unless you're Mother Teresa).

When you are happy that your pup has understood the training and is consistently toileting outside, you can scale down on the treats, but there is no harm in randomly rewarding them as they grow older!

Also, make sure that any accidents are cleaned up as quickly as possible with a cleaning product that includes enzyme cleaning in its solution. If accidents are not appropriately cleaned up, it can be much harder for your pup to understand where to toilet, which can result in a regression in toilet training.

From time to time, blind dogs can regress in this training. When this happens, just start from scratch and go easy on yourself. Life is an ongoing learning journey!

If you are doing absolutely everything right, timing the rewards correctly, and keeping the experience positive, but your dog *still* hasn't understood, it might not be your fault.

For Caitlin, this was precisely the situation she found herself in with her dog Freddy. She was doing everything right, but nothing was changing. She began to wonder if this was due to Freddy being blind or being a boy. Then, after 18 months of this, Caitlin came across a Facebook post about a similar situation, but in which the dog struggled with toilet training due to anxiety. When teaching Freddy to go to the toilet outside, he would pace for long periods and lick Caitlin's hands, but not wee. She initially thought it was a blind dog behaviour, but after seeing the post and speaking to her vet about it possibly being anxiety-related, her life turned around completely. Freddy began taking anxiety medication, and indoor toileting became a thing of the past.

Other medical issues that could cause your pup to struggle with toilet training could be urinary tract infections (UTI), ectopic ureters (a congenital disability), IBD, parasites, food hypersensitivity, urinary stones, neurological pain, and brain inflammation.

A visit to your veterinarian will help rule out or find the cause of your struggles, so don't be too harsh on yourself if things aren't progressing as they should!

12

Chewing

You now have a better understanding of how your special pup can be toilet trained; you've got this!

The next thing your wonder dog will do is chew up the house. This is a completely normal behaviour that you can address without sacrificing your furniture and shoes.

The first thing to do is to understand why this behaviour occurs.

Every single dog needs to chew; it's a natural instinct that also serves to explore their environment, and as a way to self-soothe themselves when they've become restless or agitated. This is not something that you can 'train out' of them without compromising their welfare, as you would be teaching them not to use a natural behaviour that they can rely on to manage their emotions.

Think of yawning as a similar behaviour. It comes naturally to you, it communicates to you that you might be in need of a nap, and it also helps to make you feel more relaxed as it releases neurotransmitters that facilitate the calm state of mind. Now imagine if you weren't allowed to yawn, ever. How frustrating would it feel? Chewing for dogs, especially young puppies, is similar to this example, so keep this in mind when managing this behaviour.

This may sound counterproductive, but what you need to do is encourage the chewing. Your young pup will be exploring his new world with his mouth, more so if they are blind, so you want to help him feel secure and confident by providing him with interesting things to chew. This will also meet his need to use his mouth. Generally speaking, if your pup has enough appropriate ways to display his natural behaviour, you will not see any inappropriate behaviours such as your house being chewed.

This can be done by using the previously mentioned 'leave it' cue. When you see your pup chewing on an inappropriate item, such as your shoe, simply use the 'leave it' cue and give them something appropriate to chew.

Appropriate chews can include a large variety of items that are either very cheap or even free! Your pet shop will have some of these, as well as online pet shops that specialise in unique dog chews, such as crocodile feet, that even dogs with sensitive tummies can enjoy.

Depending on the age of your puppy, you will need to be careful how hard the chews are, as some may be too hard on their young teeth and may cause them to fracture or even break. Soft chews can be bully sticks, cow/pig ears, tendons, bone marrow chews (the dehydrated types), pig noses, shark fins and tails and many more. The general rule is that if you can't leave a nail imprint on the treat, it's too hard for your pup. When they are older and if they are a large breed, they may do well with harder treats such as cow hooves, goat feet, and deer horns, but there have been cases of dogs fracturing their teeth on chews such as these, so supervise them if you choose to offer these to them.

There are also cheaper ways to meet their chewing needs, such as giving them a raw carrot or cutting up some apples and pears.

Sticks can splinter and lodge themselves in your dog's mouth without you even noticing, so be careful if your pup is a stick fan and monitor their mouth frequently.

Plastic chews, such as Nylabone and Bene Bone, are also good options for your teething pup. They don't leave as much of a mess, but they can be quite pricey, and it's not always a guarantee that your pup will like them.

Offer your pup as many chewable options as possible, but also be prepared for accidents!

Jellyfish's wall art

Jellyfish loved chewing our shoes. The strong smell must have attracted him to them, so we had to hide all our shoes in secure locations. He also went after the leather couch, the fabric couch, and at one point even the walls!

While we were constantly supervising him for toilet training, we also used that time to teach him what he could and couldn't chew. If he was chewing on the couch, we would sometimes slide in one of his chewy toys in front of him, and he would swap for it right away. The more he practised the wanted behaviour of chewing appropriate items, the less he chewed on the furniture and walls. Some items are still high risk, such as fluffy slippers and socks. I can imagine it's also hard for him to distinguish between his soft toys and household items such as pillows and people's stuffed toys. Keep this in mind, as well as how your pup's blindness affects his ability to differentiate between chewing items. All you have to do is keep encouraging him to chew on his own items, and eventually, this will be an issue of the past.

A little note on guilt.

Dogs do not feel guilt. They do not have a moral compass as we do, and they certainly don't contemplate if their actions are morally right or wrong.

This is a very common misconception that people observe when they find their dog chewing on their shoes. They report that the dog knows she's done something wrong because she will crouch, lower her ears, and overall "look guilty". In reality, your dog is displaying these behaviours as she can tell from your tone (or body language, for sighted dogs) that you are not happy. You might even be scaring them. As dogs have evolved to resolve issues in calm and cooperative ways, they will look "guilty" and less threatening so that you don't hurt them. This is the case whether you have or have not hurt them in the past. Dogs pick up on these subtle changes in our bodies, so they certainly know when we are about to give them unpleasant consequences. Even yelling can be so scary and aversive to your blind dog that they give you the "guilty" look. Next time you catch them doing something you don't like, observe your body language and tone, and try to resolve the situation in a more calm way. After all, is the loss of a shoe or a hole in the sock such a big deal?

13

Resource guarding

When you are teaching your pup what she can and can't chew on, you may run into an issue in the form of resource guarding. Simply put, this means that your dog doesn't want to let go of his resource and feels threatened if someone comes up to him while he has something important (to him).

What each dog finds important is unique to them. I met a dog once who was a serious resource guarder and would protect everyday household items such as tissues.

Resource guarding can come up at any age in any dog, so if you notice this behaviour in your new pup, there are things you can do to help him.

The reason your dog is displaying this behaviour can be due to fear and anxiety: fear of having his precious resource taken away, and anxiety about having to be vigilant and protect his belongings from you or others.

We can observe this behaviour in children as well. For example, not too long ago, it was common to teach young children to share their toys no matter what. You would be supervising some toddlers playing, when suddenly one comes up and snatches a toy off another child. The child starts crying and may lash out physically to get his toy back.

In this case, some parents may encourage the child to share and let the other child take the toy. This teaches the child whose toy was taken that no resource is safe, and he must hide them, so he isn't made to share them when he doesn't want to. More recently, knowledge in the early childhood development has changed, and we now know that sharing is not mandatory and can even be detrimental to a child's wellbeing (Paton, 2018).

You wouldn't be happy if your friend took that burger you've been looking forward to all day, so why do we think it's okay to do so to children and dogs? We all have a right to look after our belongings and things we care for deeply; it's time that we include dogs in this equation.

When your dog is chewing on something inappropriate, like your shoe, as difficult as this is, please don't snatch it away. You must replace the resource with something better, swap it for something that your dog will value even more. If you constantly take your dog's resources away, you will teach her that nothing is safe from you and that she must protect these items. If you instead swap a resource with a better one, your dog will not worry about having you in his space, and no, he won't intentionally chew up the wrong things just to get something better.

Resource guarding is a serious behaviour that can escalate quickly and, unfortunately, if it gets too far, can lead to euthanasia of an otherwise healthy dog. This is because your dog will do whatever he needs to do to protect his precious item, even escalating to biting, which can be even more significant for the very young and elderly.

Most dogs who are euthanised every year is due to behavioural issues such as aggression and resource guarding (Hitchcock et al., 2024, Yu, Fawcett, & McGreevy, 2021), so if you can prevent your dog from feeling this anxiety around resources, you will set him up for success.

If you're struggling with this and things aren't improving, please reach out to a force-free trainer near you. This may just change your life.

14

Resting

Some shelter dogs will come into your house without prior 'home' experience, meaning they won't know when it's time to rest or even *how* to relax. I can only imagine how Jelly felt in his kennel, having his sleep area near his meal area and his toilet. There was no possibility of his having learned any home skills, and with all the barking dogs in the nearby kennels, he didn't know how to rest. When he came home the first month, he didn't stop at all during the day. He was so excited about his new home and all the fun things he could do! He had toys, chews, and people who would engage with him and play with him; there was no time to rest! Having never had a dog like him, I assumed that he would eventually become tired and start sleeping during the day. This didn't happen accidentally, and we had to do some work around creating this behaviour.

You might have noticed that Jelly is a mixed breed. However, after a DNA test, we discovered he was 17% border collie. His other breeds included Australian cattle dog, Great Dane, and Pit bull. He is a wonderful mix of herding and guard breeds, which affect his personality and instincts. This means that rest is even harder for Jelly to achieve naturally, as his DNA encourages him to be on the move, on guard, and alert. Whenever he would settle down and someone would stand up, he would also get up and follow them.

We allowed this behaviour because we wanted to encourage him to be independent and explore as much as he needed to become comfortable in his new home. Eventually, he stopped getting up and started sleeping through the day.

Rest is essential for all dogs, but especially so for puppies who are growing at an incredibly fast rate. Puppies and young adults need more sleep than adult dogs, and if you've ever come across an over-tired toddler, something similar happens when a young dog is over-tired. Their self-control and some learned skills go out the window, and they may return to nibbling at your hands or chewing the couch.

On the other hand, too much rest (especially if it is forced) does not give your dog enough time to meet his needs. This may also result in restlessness and undesirable behaviour, so it's a fine line to walk when addressing the question of sleep.

There are many ways to teach rest; it's a skill that can be taught like sitting or loose-leash walking!

A spontaneous teaching method is to always have some treats in your pocket or on your person so that you can easily access them to tell your dog that you like what they are doing. As soon as they lie down, sit down, or even stand quietly and in a relaxed manner, give them a treat. Reward the calm, but do not do so in an excited manner that will get your dog riled up and break his rest. If your pup becomes excited at the presence of food, you can reward his calm behaviour by gently stroking or brushing him if he enjoys it.

Crates and x-pens can also be used to indicate to your pup that it's rest time. Make it super cozy, with blankets and a comfortable mat, so they can feel relaxed and eventually doze off.

To make this space more inviting, consider spraying some Adaptil spray. This spray is a synthetic dog pheromone smell that mother dogs produce and that calms the puppies.

We can't smell it, and some people have not noticed it make any difference, but it's still worth trying if your pup struggles. You can also try adding some calming powders to his dog food to help his system relax and help him adapt to his new home.

Our method included all of the above; however, we already had a routine that included a calm part of the day where everybody would sit down and do their work. The middle of the day was this for us, and this calmness encouraged Jelly to join us in a short rest. After a few months, he joined us in the routine and started resting from 10 am to 4 pm, and after a few more months, his body became used to resting during the day, and it's now quite a strong habit.

15

Walking

Walking a blind dog *is* possible and very rewarding for both your pup and you. All you have to do is be her eyes, lead her away from obstacles, and guide her in a safe way.

The first time you take your blind dog for a walk will be a learning experience for both of you. Depending on the location of the walk, you may not be able to zone out or have a 'normal' walk, as you will have to be her eyes to keep her safe.

Make sure you have comfortable and well-fitting equipment before you walk out the door, and keep the experience as positive as possible, especially if your pup is a little nervous. If you can, wait at least a week before taking her out so she can settle in and get to know you without being overwhelmed with information. However, if you have a bundle of energy like we did, a walk earlier in the process might just be what you need!

The first time we took Jelly for a walk, he was careful where he walked, and our walk was very slow. He sniffed everything and didn't know how to walk on a suburban street. Managing the roads, trees, and sidewalks was something that he learned each time we went out.

We quickly understood that a few more cues were needed for outside time, and that teaching 'careful' in the house was a huge advantage on our walks. We started using 'not there' for when he wanted to sniff in an area that was unsafe or tricky to get to. With encouragement, he would leave it and continue our walk, so eventually he understood the meaning of the word.

Earlier in the book, we spoke about using 'up' and 'down' for stairs. With unfamiliar stairs, we will use the predictor word and then the cue, which would look something like saying 'ready...up/down' to give him time to process and prepare for the steps. You will need to get the timing right so that it's not too early and your pup looks like a fancy dressage horse, and not too late, where he will stumble over the step.

We also included directional cues such as 'right', 'left', and 'this way'.

The cue, 'this way', means going toward the leash pressure or my voice if he is off lead. This can also help avoid obstacles, especially on those days when you are so tired that distinguishing right from left is a little too much. I
t doesn't communicate your intentions as clearly as right and left do, but both are good to know, especially if your blind pup is being walked by another person who doesn't know much about blind dogs. The cue 'this way' is commonly used in daily dog training and walks, so it is easier for your blind pup to understand if this situation ever arises.

Leash pressure is another wonderful thing that helps to guide your pup on walks. For us, no leash pressure means the coast is clear, you can go wherever you want, and you will be safe.

Light pressure with specifically more tension on one side can mean moving slightly away from the current path to avoid an obstacle. Sudden pressure can indicate an unexpected obstacle or something dangerous up ahead. We will have a tight lead when walking on narrow paths where we have to walk past people, so he understands to stay close and that he has limited freedom of movement at that moment.

For us, the leash is akin to holding hands. Do you remember being a child and holding your parents' hands when going for a walk? Did you feel safe knowing that you could feel them and that you wouldn't get lost in the mall because you trusted your parents to guide you around safely? It's the same principle with a leash. Treat it as if you are holding hands with your dog, and you will come to realise how many subtle ways of communication can be achieved through it.

The above scenario does not fit every blind dog on every walk. Leash pressure can be aversive for some dogs, even if you did everything right!

Maisie, the blind mini-Pomeranian, spent the first 3 years of her life living in a metal crate where she was used for breeding. It is unknown precisely what her experience was like in those early years, but whatever happened to her caused her to find leash pressure aversive. She still enjoys exploring the outdoors with her guardian Kat, and her adopted sister Bella, but she does so from the comfort of her pram.

Trauma can display itself through many behaviours, and sometimes these cannot be changed through training. They can be eased with time and patience, so don't feel disheartened if your blind dog can't walk on a lead. There are always multiple ways of doing something right; we just have to get creative about it!

Be prepared for your walks to be *very* slow in the beginning. Your pup will explore everything thoroughly with his nose, so don't rush him; instead, take the time to just be in the moment with him.

Remember to keep your pup safe from other dogs and people who might scare him. His first walks need to be positive and fun to build confidence and trust in his environment, so don't be afraid to put distance between others and yourselves in this sensitive period.

Hear No Evil, strongly recommends advocating for your dog on a walk and not allowing strangers to come up and pat your dog. There are a few reasons for this.

When people come up to pet a dog, they usually pet the head. Generally, dogs don't enjoy being patted on the head.

I don't know of a single person who enjoys this either. This becomes much more important with blind dogs, as they can't see the pat coming, and the head is a very sensitive body area. Even if you warn your dog that he is about to be patted on the head, you can't predict how the person will pat him. Will it be a scratch or a tap? Will they be gentle or too rough for your dog?

I like to think of blind dogs as fish. Stay with me, this will make sense!

Fish are amazing in a variety of ways, but one of the most incredible things about them is their ability to sense water temperature changes and current changes with their skin. Their skin is so sensitive that they can instantly take in all this information! Your blind dog is the same (apart from the gills and scales), and their skin is susceptible to changes in their environment as they have had to adapt to living without sight. They can feel the wind temperature and direction, its force, even your hand movements if they are close to him. Patting a blind dog must be done gently, and we can't rely on strangers to know this.

If your dog has eye issues or you suspect they might, any touch to the head will be painful for them. Conditions such as glaucoma, where there is extreme pressure buildup inside the eyes, are painful within themselves, let alone if they are touched on the head!

Furthermore, if you are teaching your dog using both verbal cues and physical touch, or if your dog is also going deaf, then random touch to the body will be confusing.

For example, Caitlin has taught Freddy to sit by gently touching his lower back. She taught him to drop with the touch of two fingers on his chest, and to stand with the touch of a single finger on his chin. Now imagine a stranger who doesn't know this and goes to touch your dog all over, "using" numerous cues at once will be incredibly confusing to your pup.

16

Calming signals

Dogs experience stress just like any other mammal, and it's up to us to understand how they display it so that we can help them.

In the beginning stages of stress, dogs will exhibit calming signals. These behaviours, such as yawning and lip licking, indicate that your dog isn't feeling comfortable. The aim of these is to resolve a stressful situation as peacefully as possible. If these don't work, and your dog's stress level rises, it can develop into behaviours such as growling and biting, as the dog feels forced to act this way to have his feelings heard.

Let's remember that *every* dog can bite; it isn't breed-specific and doesn't always relate to their past. Of course, some dogs may have learned to jump through the stress ladder and choose growing and biting as one of their first options instead of trying other ways. There are also those dogs who have been punished for growling and, as such, have learned to bite without warning, as their warning system was undesirable to their humans.

It's essential to remember this when learning your blind dog's communication methods, as you will quickly understand if they display only a few calming signals, and if the situation hasn't resolved, go on to a more assertive choice. Or maybe it takes a lot of stress to push your dog well past their comfort zone and into a red area.

Hopefully, you will never be faced with a situation where your dog feels this frustrated and uncomfortable, but just to be sure, let's learn a few essential ways that dogs send calming signals to other dogs and people.

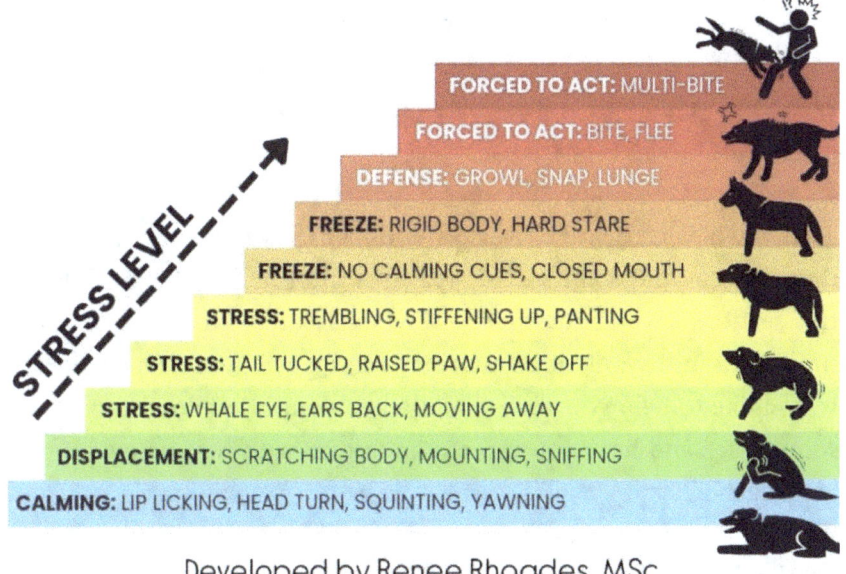

Canine communication

In the book 'On Talking Terms with Dogs: Calming Signals,' author Turid Rugaas explains the intricate world of canine communication using calming signals.

Interestingly, these communication methods are not exclusive to dog-to-dog interaction; they are a way for humans to communicate and maintain harmony with their dogs too.

Simply put, calming signals include a variety of vocal and body language cues that dogs use as a social skill to avoid conflicts and cut off aggression.

It sounds complicated, but let me reassure you that you have already observed some, if not all of the signals used by dogs.

Have you ever come up to pet a dog, only for them to roll over on their back and expose their belly to you? Have you ever stroked a dog on their head and noticed them licking their lips? These are two easily observable calming signals that dogs use to communicate their emotional state to us and ask us kindly to slow down or even stop the interaction.

If you haven't heard of Rugaas' book, I highly recommend you pick it up one day and embrace the wealth of information she provides. In this section, I won't summarise the book as that would be unfair to the author, nor would it be my aim to discuss all the signals. Instead, I would like to help you understand when your blind dog is asking for some space and how you can communicate with him using his own language.

Head turning/look away.

Head turning is a subtle movement that aims to communicate to an approaching person or dog to calm down. This can be observed when a person, for example, approaches the dog head-on and forces physical interaction on them. It's a little trickier with a blind dog, as they try to communicate their discomfort in a particular situation, the other party may not clearly understand it. After all, blind dogs move their heads more often than sighted dogs to gather information from their surroundings, so that it can be easily misunderstood as a calming signal. To make matters even more tricky, the head turning can be as subtle as your pup 'looking' in another direction, or as obvious as him turning his face completely to one side.

Try to notice this next time you are with your dog. If you are petting her and she begins turning her head, slow down the petting or even stop altogether. Does she walk away, grateful for your understanding of what she was asking, or does she face back to you and lean into your body for more pats?

You can even use this body language yourself to communicate to your pup that something is making you uncomfortable. For example, if you are not a fan of having your face licked but your pup is, try moving your face or whole head away from her as she tries to lick you and see what she does. She might understand your intentions more clearly than saying things like "no" and "stop."

Lip licking

This one is perhaps the easiest signal to identify in a dog. When a dog feels uncomfortable, he may communicate this with a lip lick first and then turn their face away to make the signal clearer. If you are speaking in a stern voice to your pup or administering ear treatment that they may not enjoy, you may notice them licking their nose frequently to tell you they don't feel comfortable with what is happening to them. It may even be more subtle than this, with only a flick of the tongue being observed in this interaction. The movement can be so quick that we often miss it or misinterpret it as them trying to kiss us when they are asking for the opposite of this.

Young puppies often display this frequent lip licking when they are being patted by multiple people who can't give them space because of how cute and fluffy they are. It's essential to respect the dog's communication and stop the unwanted behaviour when they ask for it.

If an interaction is a want and not a need, stopping it when you observe a lip lick will tell your dog that you understand and respect their feelings. You will be amazed how quickly trust between you two will grow once you learn to communicate with them!

Humans can absolutely use this signal to communicate back to their dog, but it may be a little awkward! We don't naturally lick our lips when we are uncomfortable (although I know some people who do), and we can't all extend our tongues to touch our noses. However, even a small flick of the tongue can communicate back to your dog that you understand them and that you might be feeling uncomfortable, too.

The benefit of using this signal is that it doesn't have to be visual. You can exaggerate a lip lick and make it loud enough for your pup to hear. And best of all, you can do this when you see them licking their nose! If your pup is feeling uncomfortable and shows it with a lip lick, you can stop the interaction and give them a lip lick back to diffuse the situation even more.

Freezing

This calming signal involves the dog stopping completely. You may observe it when another dog runs up to them or when they are spoken to in a loud, angry voice. Although this method is used to calm the situation, it can be harder for us to display it to a blind dog. With this signal, it's more important for us to be aware of it in our dogs than using it ourselves.

Play bow

When two dogs who don't know each other very well meet for a play, you may notice one (or both) of them stretching their front feet in front of them and lifting their bottoms in the air. This signal is quite context specific, as a play bow can mean your pup is trying to get a dog to play, or it can tell that they are trying to diffuse a stressful situation. Your pup may display this as a calming signal if they are still in the position instead of jumping around after having done the play bow. Additionally, if they remain in that position and turn their heads, it's more of an indicator that they are uncomfortable.

Jellyfish uses this signal often with other dogs when he tries to get them to play. As he can't see their body language, he relies on his ability to convince them to play with him. The wonderful thing about Jelly doing this is that he also adds vocalisations. For example, when he wants to play with a dog and goes into a bow, he will accompany it with a play growl and a series of 'woofs'. When he is stretching from a long nap, he doesn't add any vocalisations, but when his intention is to calm a situation, he will let out a groan and turn his face away.

Not all dogs will add vocal cues to this, so it's important to see the context of the situation to understand the meaning of the behaviour.

We can also use this signal by simply stretching our arms to the floor. I will usually add a groan, like one that Jelly does to respond to his calming signal. This is quite natural for us too, when we stretch to release tension, we usually have a vocal component, so realistically we already use this signal ourselves!

Yawning

Yawning is an interesting signal that is usually accompanied by a noise. You may observe your dog yawning when stressed or uncertain in situations such as the vet's office, going on a car ride, or being patted and wanting a break. Your dog may even use several signals at once, such as looking away, lip licking and finally yawning, to communicate how uncomfortable they are in that moment. We can respond to this by yawning and remembering to exaggerate it by adding a noise for our blind dogs to understand.

There are certainly more calming signals that dogs use, such as softening their eyes, slowing down their movements, and sniffing. We can't repeat all of these signals, and our blind dogs may not even be able to display them all, such as when a dog's eyes have been removed. However, it's important to be aware of the ones that your individual dog is displaying and understand that they may be a little different from how sighted dogs present them.

17

Enrichment

When people think about enrichment, they usually picture something like a snuffle mat or a Kong stuffed with food. These *are* examples of enrichment, but only one type.

These are the five types of enrichment.

Social: socialising directly or indirectly with a member of their species, or another species.

Physical: using an environment to encourage physical movement.

Nutritional: varying your dog's diet by providing different and nutritious food. Also encompasses varying feeding methods to encourage natural behaviours.

Occupational: encourages problem-solving skills by using challenges that mimic natural behaviours.

Sensory: stimulating your dog's senses by introducing new sounds/smells/textures.

In the following chapters, we will discuss four of these types, as occupational enrichment is a part of all others. For example, using a snuffle mat meets your dog's nutritional enrichment needs, but it also gives your dog a job to do, which is what occupational enrichment is all about.

But before we dive in and explore these individually (with blind dogs in mind), let's define this term and understand why it's so important.

In the book "Canine Enrichment for the Real World", Allie Bender and Emily Strong explain that enrichment is far more than just food puzzles. It's the process of finding out an individual dog's needs and structuring an environment that meets those needs. This will depend on a large variety of factors such as age, breed, physical and mental health, and your ability to meet those needs.

For example, if you have a border collie with high herding needs but you work 5 days a week and only walk her once on the weekend, it's safe to say that the dog's needs are not being met. I'm not here to judge your life choices; many tricky situations can be managed with time and patience. And this is what we're doing now, learning how to manage your new situation and ensure you have the skills and knowledge to begin the journey.

Before you can meet your dog's needs, you need to know what they are. Try to watch your dog a little more today, see what they do at home, outside, and on a walk. Do they go through the garbage (occupational enrichment: scavenging games), have constant zoomies around the backyard (physical: running), or prefer to sleep in the sunny spot all day (physical: resting)? These behaviours display their needs and give you ideas on how to meet them. If your pup's needs are not being met, they will meet them themselves, and it may not be in a safe or acceptable way.

Dogs bred for sniffing out prey, such as beagles and spaniels, have an ingrained need to fulfil these natural behaviours, which may look like going through the trash and digging up the compost. Once you start encouraging this behaviour with safe outlets, such as snuffle mats, nose work games and puzzles, the undesirable behaviour will stop.

As in the example above, most of the activities we will cover in these chapters overlap. You can focus on meeting your dog's physical enrichment when you take her for a run, but you'll also be meeting her social and occupational needs simultaneously, even if that wasn't your aim.

It's pretty difficult to keep the different types of enrichment closed off in their little boxes, so you will notice how some overlap or become a part of another type of enrichment.

Before you jump in and learn about enrichment, do keep in mind that you don't have to do them all every day. You can create a weekly schedule if you're someone who likes to organise things, or you can spontaneously do them when you have the capacity.

Basically, the reason there are different terms for different types of enrichment is to ensure that we remember to meet their needs as often as possible. Chances are, you are already doing some of this daily and not thinking about it as enrichment.

Blind dogs are also not born knowing how to safely meet their own needs in a human-led world. So, let's learn about their needs and some creative ways of meeting them.

18

Nutritional enrichment

When people hear the word "enrichment", they usually expect to see food puzzles and intricate ways of hiding food in boxes and around the house. This is definitely a type of enrichment, but it's not all. These examples are a part of nutritional enrichment and can also be classified as occupational enrichment, as your dog is working on a task that they find rewarding.

Puzzles such as these are beneficial to all dogs, but especially so for working dogs, scent hounds, and small hunting breeds. These are your spaniels, retrievers, herding dogs, beagles and terriers. They were bred by humans for specific roles, such as sniffing out and retrieving shot-down ducks, and even if they no longer live in such an environment where this role is needed, their instincts are still there and need to be met.

There are many items on the market for meeting this specific need, and many can be costly. But nutritional enrichment is simply about a dog using his nose to find food, not about purchasing hundreds of items from popular brands that promise that they are selling exactly what you need. Having said that, there is nothing wrong with purchasing puzzles, snuffle mats and balls and using them on top of handmade ones. Your dog won't judge you for using toilet paper rolls instead of a fancy puzzle.

Take a look around your house, I'm certain that when you finish reading this section, you'll be amazed at just how many things you already have to create a fun enrichment experience for your pup.

Cardboard is by far my favourite thing to use. It's versatile as it comes in many forms, it can be free, and it can sometimes even hold interesting smells from the things that it was used to hold.

Think pizza boxes from last night's takeaway. They hold the smells of the food that was in it, and if you put some treats in there, your pup is going to be overjoyed! For those of us who don't like the crust, you can even just leave it in the box for your dog to find.

Rolls of toilet paper and hand towels are also a great choice for this. You can bend the edges in of one side, put some treats in, and then close the other end. Your dog will have fun figuring out how to get the treat inside. Will she shred it? Maybe she'll be more methodical and will find a way of unbending the edges. Maybe the cardboard will become wet and fall apart from his chewing on it. The fun part for them is often the working out of how to get to the treat, and not so much the treat itself.

You can make 10 (or more!) of these and put them in a large box for your dog to sift through. You can leave them open and put them standing up inside the holes of an egg carton or a box, then drop some treats in there and give them to your dog. The egg cartons themselves can be used in this game, as you can hide treats in the egg holes and close the box (even tape it shut to make it extra tricky).

You can also make some small holes in the sides of the closed toilet paper roll, so your dog has to push and roll it to get the treats out. There are many wonderful and strange things that can be done with toilet paper rolls, so make sure to keep them around!

Boxes pair very well with pieces of cloth or shredded paper, as these act as a barrier for your dog to get the treats.

Leave the boxes open when you are first starting out with this type of enrichment, as we don't want to discourage your dog from trying to figure out the puzzle. When she is confident with these, try close the tops and watch as she figures out a way to get to the treats.

In the world of dog sports, there is a competitive sport that uses boxes and a specific scent.

Scent work training begins with either training in a class setting or on your own using food hidden in boxes. The difficulty then moves up to odour searches, where the dog has to find a smell (birch, anise, clove or cypress), and it is at this level that you can start competing against other teams. The uniqueness of this sport doesn't end there, as dogs trial one at a time, never interacting with other dogs, which means it's available for dog-reactive dogs to participate.

Some scent work organisations allow for modified rules, so be sure to check with them if you are interested in participating in this sport.

If the competition is on lead, you can help guide her near the boxes and keep her from touching them.

Scent work doesn't have to be about competing, though, and even attending a few classes can be extremely beneficial to you as a team. Most importantly, it's a great way to bond with your dog and teach him something new, even if you never go to competitions.

There are other household items that are useful in a food enrichment activity.

If you have a muffin tin and some tennis balls, you can create a fun enrichment activity with them. Simply put some treats in the tin and cover them up with the balls, so your dog will have to push the balls away or pick them up to get to the treat.

Muffin tin enrichment idea

ASPCA, 2025

Before I learned about food enrichment, I had no idea how many ways there were to fold a towel. You can roll it, fold it sideways, just fold the corners, square fold it, etc. The treats will stay hidden in the towel for your dog to work out how to reach. To make it even more tricky, hide the folded towel in a box!

Paper bags, old clothes, empty milk bottles, pillows, blankets and your own furniture can all be used in this game. To make this need even simpler to meet, you can just sprinkle your dog's food around the house and ask her to find them. This can extend your mealtime and be enjoyable for your dog too!

The main thing to remember when meeting your dog's nutritional needs is not just the delivery, which is what we've just gone over, but also the quality and quantity of the food you are giving.

If you are giving your dog with pancreatitis treats that are highly fatty, it won't be beneficial to him and can cause him harm. Therefore, the activity won't be in his best interest even if he enjoys searching for the treats. So, make sure to use appropriate treats for these games, and don't overdo it with the quantity!

19

Social enrichment

Dogs, like humans, are social creatures that thrive in environments where they can interact with members of their species and other social creatures. This is why social enrichment is so important to them; it's a way to meet their biological need, similarly to us going out on a Friday night to catch up with our friends after a long week. For some, it's a must.

When people think of social enrichment, they often think about busy places such as the dog park and dog-friendly cafes. These are certainly options to meet your dog's social needs, but they are not the only ones.

For some pups, other dogs and people can trigger a worrying emotional response, ranging from fear to over-excitement. If you are not sure how your dog is with other dogs and people, it's best to stay away from busy places and start slow.

Simply going for a walk can create an opportunity for your pup to interact with and 'see' others. Alternatively, go for a drive and watch how your dog responds when he scents people walking around outside. Does he bark at them, whine, or do nothing? All these behaviours can give you clues to how he feels about other people.

If you have friends who have friendly dogs, you could organise a playdate with them and observe how your pup interacts with the other dog. I wouldn't recommend going to the dog park with your blind pup, as you don't know what kinds of people and dogs are there and how they will react to your dog. This is true for all other dogs as well; however, it is more of an issue for blind dogs.

You may have noticed that your blind dog doesn't communicate quite like sighted dogs do. He may be unable to greet other dogs appropriately and instead walks into them head-on or from the side. He may not be able to understand if another dog doesn't want to play, and even mistake 'go away' signals for 'let's play' signals. He may be busy following a certain smell or chasing a ball that he doesn't realise he's about to step onto a dog that is lying down enjoying the sun. You will need to be vigilant and keep your blind dog safe when meeting his social needs, as even one negative incident can cause irreversible damage to your dog's confidence and resilience.

Jellyfish was born with eyes, so although other dogs found him a little loopy in his interactions, they would still engage with him and play. I can only assume that because he looked seemingly 'normal' to other dogs, they didn't find him threatening or worrying. In fact, it took our second dog, Clyde, a whole 5 days to realise that Jelly was blind. After that, he changed his tactics and would play hide and seek very differently from how he did before.

When Jellyfish was 7 months old, he developed glaucoma in his left eye and needed to have it removed. When we returned to the vet clinic to have his stitches removed and walked outside, a dog got loose in the car park and attacked Jelly. This was a freak accident in a place that I would normally consider to be quite safe, and the dog had never displayed aggressive behaviour towards other dogs before. Jelly was attacked by a friendly dog.

Thankfully, he was okay and managed to escape with some minor grazes to his neck, but not all dogs are so lucky. This is just my theory, but I believe the dog that attacked Jelly saw that he was missing an eye, she maybe even picked up on his strange body language which she found to be threatening. It's not her fault, and we can't control what other dogs find threatening so it's up to us to keep our dogs safe.

At 9 months, Jelly needed his other eye removed also due to glaucoma, and since then, we have been more careful about how we meet his social needs with other dogs. We have playdates with known friendly dogs and visit the dog park during quiet times when it's empty. Even letting your dog sniff an area where there have been many dogs and people, like a dog park, is extremely beneficial to them, and there is nothing that you have to do! We haven't touched on this yet, but this is also an example of a way that you can meet their sensory enrichment.

However, social enrichment doesn't always have to mean direct interaction with another dog or person, it can mean just 'watching' the world go by, or meeting a dog across the fence, or even being surrounded by dogs on lead/in a crate (such as at a dog show or training class) but not interacting with them. These can be achievable options if your pup is reactive to other dogs and/or people, and you can dial it down even more by just having relatives visit your pup to provide some social enrichment.

If you have a reactive dog, it is still possible to meet their social needs in a way that is enjoyable and safe for them. Suppose they have no issues with scenting people across the street, that still counts as social enrichment. If your dog is older and can't walk very far, a short walk or a stroll in a pram is also social enrichment (and sensory).

Dog sports and training classes are another great way of meeting your dog's social needs, while teaching both him and you how to navigate it safely together. These environments are a great choice, especially as in training classes dogs don't usually interact without supervision from a trainer, and it teaches your pup that she doesn't always have to say hi to everyone and can just be.

We have found training classes to be incredibly valuable in this regard, as Jelly loves other people and dogs so much that he is always trying to say hello to them. We also learned that his lack of eyesight doesn't affect his training ability at all! We successfully completed adolescent classes and basic obedience, where he even learned how to go to his mat just by relying on smell.

There are also some dog sports that are blind-dog friendly and very enjoyable. Jellyfish and I compete in SprintDog, which is similar to the American Fastcat. All he has to do is chase a lure for 100 meters. We have found it to be a supportive environment and a great opportunity for Jelly to let out his energy in an enjoyable way, as well as meet other dogs from different states and play with them. This type of activity also meets your dog's physical enrichment, which we will discuss in the following section.

Lastly, I would like to touch on the subject of doggy daycare.

This is a relatively new phenomenon that has grown incredibly over the last few years. Daycare *is* a way to meet your dog's social (and physical) needs, as their social interactions are monitored, and staff can arrange groups based on the dogs' personalities and play styles.

However, it may still be more of a risk for a blind dog.

Firstly, a member of staff has to always be watching him to make sure he doesn't walk into a potentially dangerous obstacle or another dog. They have to watch how other dogs react to him, and if done inappropriately, social interactions can lead to serious dog attacks and loss of life. If this is an option that you are exploring, speak to the staff and find out if they would be comfortable managing your pup by placing him in smaller groups, an area with minimal obstacles, and with dogs that don't mind your pup's awkward behaviour. When done correctly, it can be a useful way to meet his needs *and* give you a break for a few hours.

20

Physical enrichment

Physical enrichment refers to activities that you can do with your dog that meet their exercise needs. Some of the activities mentioned in the previous section can be used to meet this need (dog sports, daycare), but there are a few more that we can explore as well.

It is absolutely possible to play with your blind dog, they are dogs first and blind second. You will need to learn to play differently with your blind dog and remember to keep it fun for them and not be stuck in a traditional idea of how dogs should play.

Jellyfish getting ready to chase the ball

A lot of blind dogs that I know love playing fetch. People often seem to be surprised when I tell them that my blind dog loves to chase balls; they don't always believe me! The ball does need to make a noise so that it's easier for your pup to track it, such as a squeaky ball or a Kong jumbler. This latter one has a smaller ball on the inside of the larger one, and it has handles so your dog can grip it. Similarly, a tug toy with a squeaker on the inside or even a bell can motivate your pup to both tug *and* fetch the toy.

There are some safety concerns when playing tug with a blind dog, namely that he can't see your hand and is probably not even thinking about it, so accidental nips will happen during this game!

A flirt pole can help with this as it encourages your pup to chase a lure, but he won't be able to play tug with it as it's not designed to be safely tugged.

If you want to start running, your dog might just be the motivator that you need to get started. Just as you can walk with your blind dog, you can certainly run and even join running groups. You shouldn't start seriously running with your dog until their bodies have fully formed to prevent joint issues in the future. It takes longer for larger breeds than smaller ones, so exercise caution and don't overdo it!

If you are competitive, canicross is a sport that can help you meet your dog's physical needs. In canicross, the dog runs in front of you and pulls you forward in the race. The equipment must be comfortable for both parties for this to be safe, but it's incredibly enjoyable, especially if your dog loves to pull.

Another sport that meets this need is agility. I haven't personally tried agility with Jellyfish, but I have taught him how to go over obstacles with a 'jump' cue, and he does know how to weave between poles. A few aspects of traditional agility training can be enough to satisfy your blind dog and keep them safe. Jumping can be extremely satisfying for them, as well as trying out new things such as going through tunnels and over A-frames or dog walks.

You can create your own obstacle course in your backyard by using second-hand or even free equipment!

There are many ways to meet your pup's physical needs that are even simpler than any that I have described above. Simply going for a new walk, in a new direction or even driving to a lovely nature reserve can contribute to meeting this need. So, play with your dog, explore new places and try out some fun classes. You won't be just expanding your dog's world, but yours as well.

21

Sensory enrichment

Sensory enrichment refers to stimulating your dog's hearing and meeting your dog's sensory needs. This is exactly what it sounds like, creating experiences that touch your dogs' senses.

Your dog doesn't necessarily have to do anything to benefit from the activity. If, for example, you choose to focus on hearing and put on some classical music, you will be meeting your dog's sensory needs, and all they have to do is enjoy it!

In our case, we only have four senses to focus on, so let's look at different ways of meeting these needs.

Hearing

As mentioned earlier, music is one way in which we can stimulate your dog's sense of hearing. Classical and Reggae music have been found to be the most relaxing and enjoyable music genres for dogs (Kogan, Schoenfeld-Tacher, & Simon, 2012), but every dog is an individual, and I have no doubt that there are some heavy metal fans out there! Finding out what genre (or even artist) your dog enjoys listening to isn't too difficult. Watch your dog's reaction when a certain genre is played. Does he continue to lie down in the room with you, or does he walk away to sleep elsewhere? Does she become agitated all of a sudden, or does she lie down next to you?

These are all clues your dog gives you to tell you how they are feeling, so watch out for them and learn what music they find most relaxing.

The volume of whatever music you choose to play should be kept quite low, as a dog's hearing is much more sensitive than ours is, and although your blind dog may enjoy listening to the song you put on, he might not be comfortable with how loud it is and walk away because of this.

Another way to meet this need is to spend some time outside with your dog. There are many sounds outside that your dog will find enjoyable and comforting. The sound of the trees moving in the wind, the birds chirping, and cars driving by may be extremely enjoyable to them.

Stimulating your dog's hearing also involves introducing them to new sounds, such as construction noises, waves at the beach, or the sound of a guitar being played. Again, watch your dog and see if they find it interesting and enjoyable, as some blind dogs with noise sensitivity can find some sounds aversive and even painful.

Touch

Touch sensations are vital to your dog's wellbeing, and many dogs love being given a gentle massage or being stroked on their belly. With a blind dog, warn them before touching them, as it might come as a surprise to them!

Keep the touch interaction gentle, without any rough massages or heavy pats. Dogs have sensitive skin, and blind dogs especially are aware of the weight of a person's pat.

Find out what areas your dog likes being touched and massage him regularly. Most dogs dislike having their ears, head, and feet touched, and will not always display it as obviously as walking away from the interaction. So, you need to be aware of the previously discussed calming signals your dog displays to understand his preferences fully. Some dogs are touch-sensitive and prefer not to be given many pats. This is entirely normal, so don't feel like you have to force any physical interaction on him if he doesn't enjoy it.

Introduce your dog to different-textured ground, such as sand, water, and mud. Even playing with a variety of toys will meet this need for novel touch sensations. Rubber toys, soft toys, and rope will each feel different in her mouth, and she will be excited about this new item and playing with you.

Smell

Everything we discussed in the Chapter, 'Nutritional Enrichment', can stimulate a dog's nose. However, you can add to these to enhance your dog's experience with smells.

If you have a little space to spare in your balcony or backyard, creating an herb garden for your dog will be incredibly interesting for them. By planting dog-safe herbs, such as chamomile, lavender, and mint, your dog can go into this little garden and smell the various herbs.

Some plants, such as oleander, tulips, and lilies, can be toxic to dogs, so research a plant before allowing your dog near it. The effects of ingesting a lily can range from vomiting to kidney failure, so if you already have some of these plants in your home, consider moving them away from where your blind dog can reach them.

Some smells, such as lavender and chamomile, can be both interesting and calming for your dog. They don't have to be planted for your dog to explore the scent, as they can be easily purchased as essential oils and diluted with some tap water. You can spray them on your dog's bedding or on a blanket first to see if they enjoy the smell.

There are smells on everything we touch, do, and bring home, so let your dog investigate your clothes and shopping when you return home. If your friends leave some clothes at home, let your dog smell them.

Lastly, don't forget about letting your dog stop and smell as much as possible during your walks. There are so many wonderful smells for them to explore on a walk, and for many, it is their favourite part of going outside.

Taste

This sense can also be easily stimulated during your nutritional enrichment activities, as you can provide them with different tasting treats.

Hiding some dry treats in a box and moist foods such as cooked chicken breast in another will excite your dog's taste buds. Alongside taste, you can also provide them with foods of different textures and temperatures. Homemade popsicles made with your dog's favourite foods are a great opportunity to stimulate those taste buds *and* cool your dog down during a hot day.

Try giving her some bone broth or peanut butter and watch her reaction. There are many dog-safe foods in our homes already, so use those before purchasing any from the shops.

22

Growing up

You might have noticed some strange changes in your puppy as they grow up. Does he suddenly prefer to listen to strangers when they ask him to sit rather than you? Have they gotten a taste for the couch again, despite all the hard work you've put in to teach him to leave it alone? These are signs that the wonderful stage of adolescence is upon you!

It's no wonder people call this the most challenging phase in your and your dog's lives. Just like a human teenager, your pup's body is undergoing major changes; their brain is being remodelled and developing very quickly. The last part of the brain that develops is, unfortunately, the frontal lobes, which are responsible for self-control. This means that it's not your fault! Your dog's brain is working so hard to finish developing that he can't help being impulsive; it's neither your dog's nor your fault.

These changes come in various intensities for different dogs, so depending on your dog's temperament, life experiences, genes, and routine, they may be barely noticeable.

On the other hand, it's also possible that these changes will be so noticeable, scary, and unexpected that you won't know what's happened to cause these new behaviours. The most important thing is to be kind to yourself and your pup.

You will both be going through some major changes, but don't forget that all this is temporary! You won't be living with an eternal teenager; he *will* grow out of it with your patience and support and become the best version of himself as an adult dog.

Let's remember that this stage comes at different ages for different dogs. In general, it begins between 6 and 8 months of age, but smaller dogs may reach the teenage stage at 6 months, while larger breeds may reach it later at 10 or even 12 months. Again, this won't last forever, only about 1-3 years.

It's not all bad news, though. While you might be struggling with simple things such as recall or getting your pup to settle, you will also have a bundle of energy who is excited about life and wants to be a part of it as much as possible. They will be curious about things they may have ignored previously, get into scuffles with other dogs as they learn appropriate social skills, and be so happy to spend time with you, working out all this jittery energy.

At this stage in a dog's life, they are often surrendered to shelters or re-homed as their family struggles to make sense of the behaviour and how to manage it appropriately. This is also when reactivity may be displayed towards things or beings with whom they have never had a problem before.

On a side note, I'm surprised that not all blind dogs are reactive. I can only imagine how unsettling it must be to not know who is going to be on the same walk as you, who will pat you, who will zoom by on their bike, and that there are construction noises nearby that weren't there before—and you can't see any of it!

That is why your skills as a handler are so important. You are there to tell her that there is a person coming, or a dog or a bike. Just help them prepare for what's coming so they don't have to feel anxious and attempt to deal with the situation on their own. That's all that reactivity is!

A dog that doesn't know how to handle a situation in any other way will do it in the way that works for him. They might bark or lunge to create space between them and the trigger. They might cower and refuse to walk so they don't have to face the potential trigger. They will do what works for them, so it's up to us to show them that there are other ways of dealing with the situation and that you're there to help them resolve it.

If you think your dog is becoming reactive, please get in touch with a certified force-free trainer near you (or even online). This is such a critical stage in your dog's life, and with kindness and patience, you will be able to come out of it together as a strong team.

When Jelly was beginning the adolescent stage, we decided to pause most of our training. In fact, we paused most of what we were doing so that he could grow and develop without any of our expectations and goals getting in the way. We stopped going to training classes and on busy walks. We invited our friends over less and instead let Jelly rest at home. We limited his interactions with strangers and unknown dogs, but we still organised some play dates and walks with his known doggy friends.

In this stage, Jelly became noise sensitive and found his voice, which meant a lot of barking at passing people and our neighbours. When sighted dogs bark at a passerby, the advice is usually to block their vision by closing the curtains or sticking an opaque film over the windows. It's a little trickier with a blind dog, as blocking sound isn't always easy.

We have found music to work well, and leaving the TV on for him when we know it's busy outside (such as when school finishes), or using a white noise machine to block out the sounds. However, when he gets stuck in a cycle of barking and can't seem to calm himself down, we intervene.

Now, this might sound a little strange, but it works for us. When Jelly barks, we hug him.

Firstly, we will go to where he's barking and walk with him for a bit to see if there's a danger (like a lizard or injured possum) to which he's alerting. If there's nothing there, and he is just walking around barking at omething we can't hear or smell, we will step in and hug him. The hugs stop him from pacing and stirring himself up more and more.

The touch and weight of the hug comforts him, quite similar to a thunder jacket or a weighted blanket for humans. He can hear my breathing, my heartbeat, and me talking to him. We give him slow, long pats and speak to him in a soft voice. This is where he will usually bring his attention to me and maybe do a yawn. That's his signal for "I'm okay now, I don't need the hug anymore."

Although Jelly finds this comforting, not all dogs will react this way. In fact, a majority of dogs don't like hugs from us. If this is the case with your dog, try just being there with him while he barks and pat him. You won't be reinforcing the barking, as it stems from an emotional state, and as you can't reinforce an emotion, the patting will only bring comfort to your dog. Most dogs will find it comforting to have you with them when they bark, especially if they're blind and think there is a danger nearby. Your presence will tell them that you believe them, and that they are safe.

After Jelly is finished with his hug, we can then call him away to an area where the sound trigger can't reach him, or put some music on. This strategy might not seem realistic in the long run, but it's helped Jelly learn how to self-regulate and stop barking, as he knows how to take a break and move away from the trigger. The other upside to this is that Jelly trusts me more and feels safe when I'm around, meaning that he will bark less and be better able to focus on me if there is a lot of noise outside. It's also helped him relax at home when everyone is at work, so next time your pup barks, try to be curious and be with him instead of trying to stop it, if yelling at a dog to stop was successful, we wouldn't have so many people struggling with their dogs barking!

Although adolescence is a time for change, there may be some things that your blind dog won't necessarily grow out of, for example, social skills.

These are hard for blind dogs to pick up on and learn, as sighted dogs have a wider assortment of communication options that rely on sight. For example, your blind pup might not see the other dog lifting his lips, having whale eyes, staring at him, crouching, or tensing. This will always be a challenge for your dog, which is why it's so important for you to be there and guide him through these situations.

Blind dogs are also really good at finding things that they aren't supposed to, which is something that sighted dogs do at this age as well, but your blind dog might not grow out of it. As their sense of smell is so exceptional, they're at a higher risk of sniffing out something dangerous (such as chocolate or medication) at all stages of their lives. Keeping dangerous items and foods away from their reach and preferably locked up is the safest way to ensure your dog is safe, even when unsupervised.

23

The end!

And with that, you have completed the book!
Thank you for sticking with me throughout this journey.

I hope that you have gained some valuable skills and feel confident in your abilities to raise a blind dog.

Your journey will have ups and downs, but it will always be so worth it.

Your dog is alive, you are alive.

One day, even the memory of the bad days will be sweet.

Trust yourself, you've got this!

Resources and further reading

Michaels, L. (2022). *The do no harm dog training and behavior handbook: Featuring the hierarchy of dog needs®*. Do No Harm Dog Training.

Rugaas, T. (2005). *On talking terms with dogs: Calming signals*. Dogwise Publishing.

Bender, A., & Strong, E. (2019). *Canine enrichment for the real world: Making it a part of your dog's daily life*. Dogwise Publishing.

Yin, S. (2011). *Perfect puppy in 7 days: How to start your puppy off right*. Cattledog Publishing.

DogZone. (2022). *Is crate training cruel?*

ASPCA. (2025). *Canine DIY enrichment*. American Society for the Prevention of Cruelty to Animals.

Skene, K., O'Farrelly, C. M., Byrne, E. M., Kirby, N., Stevens, E. C., & Ramchandani, P. G. (2022). Can guidance during play enhance children's learning and development in educational contexts? A systematic review and meta-analysis. Child Development, 93(4), 1162–1180.

Weisberg, D. S., Hirsh-Pasek, K., Golinkoff, R. M., Kittredge, A. K., & Klahr, D. (2016). Guided play: Principles and practices. Current Directions in Psychological Science, 25(3), 177–182.

Mahler, K. (2017). *Interoception and toileting*. ERIC.

Paton, M. (2018). *Sharing is caring – or is it?* CELA.

Yu, K., Fawcett, A., & McGreevy, P. D. (2021). Mortality due to undesirable behaviors in dogs aged three years and under attending veterinary clinics in Australia. Animals, 11(2), 493.

Hitchcock, M. E., Jeffery, U., Toukhsati, S. R., & McGreevy, P. D. (2024). *Behavioral reasons for euthanasia in dogs: Prevalence, risk factors, and implications.* Frontiers in Veterinary Science, 11, Article 1387076.

Kogan, L. R., Schoenfeld-Tacher, R., & Simon, A. A. (2012). *Behavioral effects of auditory stimulation on kenneled dogs.* Journal of Veterinary Behavior, 7(5), 268–275.

About the author

Anastasia is the lucky human who lives with her blind dog, Jellyfish, and his adopted brother, Clyde. She enjoys learning about dog behaviour and training and is especially interested in raising awareness about reactive and blind dogs.

She has published a picture book titled " Zoodle Needs Some Space," which follows the life of a reactive dog named Zoodle and aims to teach children and adults about reactivity. In her personal life, she works as a veterinary nurse in general practice and emergency and enjoys trying out new classes and competitions with her dogs.

www.ingramcontent.com/pod-product-compliance
Lightning Source LLC
Chambersburg PA
CBHW071247070526
44583CB00017B/2367